FLAVOURS OF THE
ORIENT

FLAVOURS OF THE ORIENT

RANI KING & CHANDRA KHAN

PIATKUS

For Mum and Dad, for
believing in their 'little girls'

© 1996 Rani King and Chandra Khan

First published in 1996 by
Judy Piatkus (Publishers) Ltd
5 Windmill Street, London W1P 1HF

A catalogue record for this book is available from the British Library

ISBN 0 7499 1678 8

Photographs by Steve Baxter
Food prepared by Oona Van Der Berg
Styling by Marian Price
Text designed by Paul Saunders
Step-by-step illustrations by Rodney Paull; decorations by Paul Saunders

Jacket photograph shows Beef Smoore, rice, Chicken Satay, Sri Lankan Hoppers, Barbecued
Duck, Fried Rice Sticks with Seafood and Vegetables, Spring Rolls and Pao

Typeset by Create Publishing Services Ltd.
Printed and bound in Great Britain by
Bookcraft Ltd, Midsomer Norton, Somerset

Contents

Acknowledgements

We would like to thank Mum and Dad for believing 'their little girls could achieve anything'; John for ruining two cars and his back lugging Tiger Lily products around for seven years; Howard for his support and encouragement; Justin, the greatest fan of our products; Neisha for being there with us right from the start; and Johnny and Julian for being patient guinea pigs for our recipes.

Also Heather and all the lovely people at Piatkus for 'nursemaiding' us through our first book, Mark Lewis and Peter Irvine of Harvey Nichols, Cyrus and Pervin Todiwala of Café Spice Namaste and Bruno Loubet of L'Odéon for their invaluable help and support.

Mum

Dad

Johnny, Justin, Neisha and Julian – our darlings

Chandra's thanks go to all whose professional advice helped make Tiger Lily a success: Ron Gardiner of NLTEC, Albert Wright of BEC, and all at NatWest. Not forgetting BT plc for being a good employer for 17 years, then releasing her to carve a new career.

Rani's thanks go to Elaine Norman and Chris Turner, Tony Shillingford, Usha Sharma, Mike Boland, Gillian Dyer and Tom Adams for their encouragement when things were difficult, and to the Department for Education and Employment who allowed her to develop her journalistic talents to the full.

Finally, our grateful thanks to Helen Hague whose news article boosted our efforts on to a waiting world, and our customers for their faithful patronage.

To all those mentioned above, and to those we have not been able to name through lack of space, goes our love!

Introduction

THIS BOOK introduces recipes from China, Malaysia, Thailand, Indonesia and Sri Lanka which can be easily followed, and cooked with the minimum of time and fuss. Or, to paraphrase Shirley Conran who freed so many of us from the tyranny of the kitchen in the seventies with the battle cry 'Life is too short to stuff a mushroom', we say 'life is too short to grate a coconut'!

Like many women today, our lives are a careful balancing act between family, work and socialising. Although we love good food we simply do not have the time to spend hours in the kitchen laboriously producing gourmet meals. All our recipes have therefore been designed to produce authentic tastes without the fuss and mystique that so often surround Oriental and South-East Asian cooking.

We hope you will enjoy trying out our recipes and that your friends and family will enjoy the results. But most of all we hope you will have as much fun reading this book as we have had writing it, and reminiscing about how it all started . . .

When asked where she was going, my sister Chandra aged just two, apparently tucked me (two weeks) under her arm firmly and said, continuing towards the lake outside the house: 'I'm going to drown the cat because it wails so much.'

This could well have been the shortest working relationship in history. However I was saved that day and lived to repay her attentions. By the time I was two myself (and Chandra just four), we had managed to inject each other with my grandfather's insulin, taken his deadly heart pills and had our stomachs pumped out, and I had (literally) given Chandra a close shave with our father's cut-throat razor. She bears the scars on her chin to this day.

Not for nothing were the servants terrified of the 'terrible twins'. However, we were always close and, as we grew, we shared an increasing love of food. Chandra's first words in Thai were 'King Kao!' (eat rice), and if set down she would immediately toddle towards the kitchen. Her legs grew so fat and her thighs forced so wide apart that her feet turned in and she was forced to wear correction boots. Much of our interest in food derived from our parents' mistaken belief that fat children were healthy children. Mother paid each of our *amahs* or nannies (there were four of them, one for each of her daughters) a bonus if we put on weight at the weekly weigh-in. It was a bit like Weight Watchers in reverse.

This resulted in them running behind us with bowls of rice balls which they would try and force-feed us, like baby birds, at every opportunity. We would shin along the almost horizontal coconut tree trunks (we lived on the beach in Sri Lanka and the fierce sea winds moulded all the trees landwards) and when our *amahs* almost managed to get to us we would bounce up and down vigorously until they fell off.

We had an idyllic childhood travelling around the world in the wake of our very glamorous parents, a Sri Lankan diplomat and Chinese film-star mother. In our early days we were cared for by a retinue of servants from whom we learnt many tricks of the catering trade. Dad's posting to the Court of St James in London, and to our exciting Embassy in Washington DC, gave us access to food cooked by the best diplomatic chefs in the world. We became used to eating smoked salmon, caviar and lobster and dining out in the best restaurants. Now we realise how very fortunate we were but then we took it much for granted. However, our palates benefited from this early exposure to gourmet food, and the combinations of unusual ingredients, prepared with imagination and panache, have influenced our own recipes.

Although we moved in very grand circles on the embassy circuit, back home we lived idyllically simple lives very close to nature. We spent wonderful days and nights eating with the fisher folk who lived in thatched palm huts on the beach outside our grand gates. We both well remember the most wonderful rice and curries which came from earthen *chatties* or round pots cooked over open fires. Also the way the men would come home in the early hours of the morning, phosphorous flying like showers of stars from the bows of their catamarans. And the thrill of seeing the myriad coloured fish which we now see in aquariums but then would be bundled unceremoniously into the nearest cooking utensil.

Our love of good food and handed-down family recipes from around the world inspired us to form our company, Tiger Lily – Oriental Fire! Specialising in the authentic tastes of Sri Lanka and the Pacific Rim (i.e. Thailand, Malaysia, Singapore and Indonesia). We launched a range of instant Oriental spice mixes, relishes and other culinary essentials, all with a shelf life of at least a year but with no additives, preservatives or colourants.

The full range of Tiger Lily products is now stocked in what is possibly the UK's premier foodmarket, The Fifth Floor of Harvey Nichols in Knightsbridge, haunt of the Princess of Wales and other celebrities. Very few visitors to London go home without visiting this world-famous store whose reputation is based on stocking the finest foods from around the world, usually produced by small family firms who, like us, are not interested in mass-produced or synthetic tastes.

Tiger Lily, it seems, has built up an ardent following of genuine 'foodies'. The Christmas 1995 edition of the exclusive Harvey Nichols' magazine, which featured meals from around the world, included Tiger Lily's Sri Lankan recipes. We also give food workshop lectures on Oriental food, and regular tastings.

Now we open our well-thumbed, hand-written recipe books and share with you the food we prepare lovingly for our friends and families. Nothing would give us greater pleasure than to see a copy of our book in your kitchen, stained, dog-eared (to mark your favourite recipe) and even scribbled in. This would show us that you are adapting the recipes to suit *yourself* and your families.

We love food, we respect food. It is our way of expressing love for our nearest and dearest, but we do not let it rule our lives. Exotic meals can be made with the minimum of effort and, to be honest, a little inventive 'tweaking'.

Using the basics found in most people's storecupboards, with a few additions, you too can replicate **the Fiery Taste of the Orient!**

THE BIRTH OF TIGER LILY

Since we started Tiger Lily, we have entered the best kitchens in the UK, met internationally recognised chefs and held our own against the finest food manufacturers in the world. We export to New Zealand and the Channel Islands, and have launched a national UK mail order business – can you wonder that we sometimes have to pinch ourselves to see if we are dreaming?

Tiger Lily products are used by Curry Club's Chef of the Year (1994 to 1997) Cyrus Todiwala of London's Café Spice Namaste Restaurant, and by Michelin-starred Bruno Loubet of the famous L'Odéon in Piccadilly. Restaurants owned by our natural 'home', Harvey Nichols, with renowned chef Henry Harris of The Fifth Floor and Foundation in the basement, use our products. We are waiting with bated breath for the OXO Restaurant, Bar and Brasserie on London's South Bank to open under the Harvey Nichols' banner and hope to supply that outlet, too.

'So, how did it all begin?' we are constantly asked. This is our story – hard to believe but true. Founded on a £5 bet, it has brought us amazing highs and lows. There have been loads of laughs, and days when we have cried with sheer exhaustion and frustration and nearly killed each other. Would we do it again? . . . Want to bet another fiver?

Rani is now a journalist and editor of a government magazine. Some six years ago, she was sent on secondment to HRH the Prince of Wales's Business in the Community (BITC) organisation as Special Initiatives Manager. Her remit was to look at ways of encouraging enterprise, especially in disadvantaged groups such as inner-city residents, women (who found it difficult to raise finance or be taken seriously when trying to set up their own businesses), and those from ethnic minorities. This was some time back and things have changed for the better since. She also wrote a guide on how to survive redundancy, and researched employee buyouts and cooperative working arrangements.

During her time with BITC she came across Duonne Alexander-Moore, a single parent from a Caribbean background who was producing a family recipe from her kitchen on a council estate in London's East End. Duonne was a fighter and inspired Rani with her story – against all the odds she was selling her 'Gramma's pepper sauce' in the most exclusive outlets in London.

Rani was telling Chandra, and eldest sister Micky, about Gramma's when, as usual, brothers-in-law John (Chandra's husband) and Michael (Micky's) began teasing her, saying she was always full of great ideas and advice so 'how come you aren't a millionaire?' (This was a favourite family jibe, along the lines of 'if you're so clever why aren't you rich?') Incensed, and united by family loyalty, the three sisters took on Michael's bet of £5 that we couldn't market our own 'secret family recipes' or run a successful business.

We chose the name Tiger Lily because Rani was born in the year of the Tiger – a sign that is fearless, enterprising, playful and successful; the king of the jungle. We hoped some of those characteristics would be reflected in our 'baby' company. We also wanted to feminise it with the flower symbol, and we still appear in public with tiger lilies in our hair and sprays of the flowers around us. Then came intense research into bottling and preserving techniques, and meetings with public health officers, trade inspectors and food laboratories. They all helped us to translate our family recipes into ones that would be commercially acceptable but would still contain no additives or preservatives, only natural ingredients made exclusively by hand, in traditional ways.

We called on the Cooperative Development Agency and, with a great deal of help and advice from Derek Oakley, registered our company as a cooperative, limited by guarantee.

Then, with a range of four relishes and two pickles, confident that we would not be killing anyone with anything we produced and that we were totally legal, we began our market research on an unsuspecting public.

Dawn would be just starting to paint the sky with delicate fingers of pink (around 5.30 a.m) when we loaded Chandra's car and set up a trestle table on nearby Duckett's Common, North London, at the regular Saturday car boot fair. Here Rani, Chandra, and her daughter Neisha, sold our small bottles with their hand-written labels. The first time we ventured out (jostling against others selling old pots, rusting parts of cars and motor bikes, clothes and assorted bric-a-brac) astonishingly we had sold out by 2pm, with customers placing orders for the following week.

After waiting some months to see if we were a five-minute wonder or if, once the novelty had worn off, we could attract repeat sales, we realised there was a genuine market for our products. We decided we were ready to brave the world beyond London N22.

Dressed to kill, Chandra, in a very expensive suit, and Rani, in a delicious wide-brimmed hat, made appointments with Harrods, Fortnum and Mason's, and the Army and Navy's food hall managers (go for the top, that has always been our motto!). We disregarded the bad omen when a passing tube train whisked Rani's hat off her head. The last we saw of it, it was heading north on the Piccadilly line. We convinced ourselves it meant that we, too, would soon be on the fast track.

We had polite refusals from the first two calls, but struck lucky on the third. Bipin Shah was an Asian and shrewd enough to realise that Tiger Lily may have been highly unusual but had commercial promise, hand-written labels or not. He took a chance, bless him, sending us away to have proper labels designed and giving us the commitment of our first order. We found an art student wandering around the same car boot fair, who agreed to design our labels. Unfortunately he was an atrocious speller. After several heated discussions he reluctantly agreed to change the word 'firey' to 'fiery' (our slogan was 'The Fiery Taste of the Orient'). We were on our way!

The next few years were hard graft, as anyone who has run a small business will know. We toured the UK at trade shows, local and national fairs, plugging our relishes and pickles. We offered tastings, little cubes of bread, crackers or fresh vegetables to try the products. And how we talked! Endless explanations of who we were, how we started, giving advice and recipes written on the back of scraps of envelopes or shopping lists to a curious and seemingly insatiable public. After many, many hours of smiling and being polite we would go out behind the stand, away from the public, scream quietly and vent our rage by kicking and jumping on as many cardboard boxes as we could find. We would then come out, composed and smiling sweetly.

Once, at the International Food Exhibition, Wembley, which attracts buyers from all over the world, the two of us were jumping up and down as usual, like demented chimpanzees, when we looked up and to our horror realised there was a balcony. With our open-top stand, we had attracted a large crowd of interested spectators!

All of us worked at this stage: Micky part-time as a midwife; Chandra as a full-time trainer with British Telecom; and Rani, by then a press officer, also full-time for the Rural Development Commission, often travelling out to the countryside. We moonlighted at weekends, and used up valuable holidays and evenings to nurture the business. There was always the elusive promise of success just around the corner – and that £5 bet – to goad us on.

We shared a kitchen at the local Caribbean Senior Citizens' centre, passed by environmental officers, to manufacture our relishes. Because of our own work commitments, Sunday was our usual production day. In the beginning it was a disaster. We forgot essential ingredients, doubled up on others, and took so long to get started that we often had to work until 2am. We would spend 12 hours making 35 bottles of pickle which we sold for £2.50 each – hardly cost-effective. We were living examples of the old saying 'too many cooks spoil the broth'!

We also had neighbours. In the main hall was a charismatic Christian group and out of respect we tried to keep the noise down. One of us would stand, ear to the door, listening for the moment when the prayers stopped and the 'hallelujahs' began. That was the cue to run the food processor, so the noise would be drowned out by the praises to God, drum rolls and organ music. We would be weak with laughter, speculating how Delia Smith would have coped! No wonder it took an age to make our products. We would also often forget to bring our special headgear (compulsory when producing food) and had to put carrier bags on our heads instead. An amazing sight indeed.

We nearly gave up when the House of Fraser (Army and Navy's owners) closed the Victoria Food Hall. It was convenient, as it was only ten minutes from where Rani worked so she could pop a Tiger Lily flower on her head and promote the products in her lunch hour. They were also our only regular customer, although the trade shows brought in ad hoc orders.

It was the last straw for Micky who left the company to start her own business. But Chandra and Rani refused to give up and took a final gamble, spending every remaining penny on one last show – the *Times* Food Show in London, in 1993.

Every year since Tiger Lily was born, Chandra, Rani and Neisha have set up stall in the Hay's Galleria, a converted London dock opposite London Bridge and the London Dungeon. Here, on the first weekend in September (the first summer month with an 'r' in its name when it is safe to eat seafood), a very up-market Seafood Festival takes place, with live music and the most wonder-ful ambience. We always cook our special prawn curry and rice, curry pancakes and seafood noodles, and catch up with customers who have become firm friends. This particular year, Anton Mosimann was signing copies of his latest book at a book shop. We very shyly put some of our relishes and pickles in a carrier bag and gave them to him, mentioning how much we loved his books and TV programmes. We told him we were going to the *Times* Show the following month and were looking forward to seeing his cookery demonstration.

Can you imagine our delight when Anton searched all through the *Times*

Show and came up to us, gave Rani a kiss, and congratulated us on the quality of our products. He said he had enjoyed them very much. We were so touched that someone of that stature would show such kindness and give us such encouragement. It gave us renewed faith and the extra strength to go on.

Opposite our stand was one five times the size, staffed by Harvey Nichols' employees from the Foodmarket. We made friends with them and fed them endless samples of our relishes on toast. Luckily for us, Peter Irvine and Mark Lewis, the buyers who were there, took an interest in our range, and were intrigued at the numbers of people queuing up to buy them. They asked us to come and see them after the show, and since then we have worked closely with Mark, developing new curry powders, mixes and other products, so that we now have over 35 items on our own shelves, and new ones regularly in the pipeline.

Also at the *Times* Show was Cyrus Todiwala of Café Spice Namaste. We have become firm friends with Cyrus, his lovely wife Pervin and two little rascal sons. We often deliver his favourite coconut sambol mix to his home address. However, there was one memorable occasion when our whole family, including Mum and Dad, went for a celebratory dinner at his restaurant (known to money dealers, traders and brokers as one of the finest Indian restaurants in the UK) and took another 'guest' through the front doors – 40kg of coconut sambol, which Cyrus was desperate for!

We came across Michelin-starred chef Bruno Loubet via Harvey Nichols again. Bruno was signing copies of his book when he spotted our range. We got a phone call to pop in and see him with some samples but we nearly didn't turn up. We thought he said his name was Bruin le Bear. Rani's son Julian convinced us it was a hoax – he (with the wisdom of a French GCSE under his belt) said no one could be called Bruno the Bear. Luckily Justin, her other son, is a gourmet and regularly entertains customers on the town. When he had finished laughing he gave us a rundown on Bruno's reputation and told us to get up there – double quick!

We trotted up to the West End with our usual tupperware pots of pickles, curries and mixes and spent some fascinating afternoons advising Bruno on how we mixed flavours and spices. He now orders regularly but, more importantly, is generous enough to allow us to use his name in promoting Tiger Lily.

We were featured in the food column of the *Daily Telegraph* newspaper (with testimonials from Mark Lewis, Bruno and Cyrus) and since then we have been inundated with requests for our products both through mail order and increased volume sales in Harvey Nichols. Rani mentioned in the article that we were thinking of writing a cookery book and within a few weeks we were discussing contracts with Piatkus Books.

So, you see, this book is the fruit of six funny, rewarding, exhausting, maddening, frustrating, ego-denting, ego-building years during which we have met the most interesting people from a range of occupations and backgrounds who nevertheless all share a real and abiding love of good food. Our baby Tiger Lily has come through all weathers and, even if we aren't millionaires by this time next year (as Del Boy is always promising little brother Rodney in *Only Fools and Horses*), we will have enjoyed the experience.

We hope you enjoy *Tiger Lily Flavours of the Orient* ... and by the way, Michael, isn't it time you coughed up that £5?!

Planning a Meal

SERVING ORIENTAL and South-East Asian meals is simplicity itself. Unlike the Western jack-in-the-box ritual, where the frazzled host or hostess is up and down all night serving three or more courses in turn, each one often requiring individual heating up, our meals are mostly placed on the table together except for the puddings. Very few of these are served hot so they can be prepared well in advance. More often, we would end the meal with a selection of refreshing tropical fruit cut into beautiful shapes.

We frequently cook the food a few days in advance (believing that curries taste better as they mature and the flavours have a chance to develop) and then heat the dishes together, in the oven or microwave, before serving. Remember to cover the dishes so the food does not dry out.

Everyone helps themselves to a little of everything, including soup. Some homes invest in a 'lazy Susan', a round serving area in the middle of the dining table which swivels round. Dishes can then be offered around the table without anyone having to move.

We prefer to eat most curry dishes lukewarm. This is very convenient, as food can be heated, dished out and left on the table to cool before your guests arrive. Sometimes the chilli heat of a curry coupled with a too-high serving temperature can be overwhelming and ruin the taste of a carefully prepared dish.

We like lots of different side dishes, plenty of vegetables and not very much meat or other protein. Our family meals include one protein dish, one vegetable dish, and a rice, noodle or flour-based accompaniment.

Although stir-frying takes only minutes, food should be served as soon as possible after cooking. We have prepared stir-fried dishes in advance and then heated them, but they are not at their best. The preparation for Chinese food is quite lengthy, especially washing and cutting the ingredients. For entertaining, our tip is to prepare everything the night before, including measuring out the ingredients on to a single tray or plate, then cover with cling film until the next day.

DRINKS

We are often asked what type of beverages go well with our meals. There are some very good Asian beers but normally a refreshing fruit-based drink is offered. Freshly squeezed lime juice, sweetened with sugar, and served in a tall glass with plenty of ice cubes, is a favourite. So is passion fruit juice, or mangoes or watermelons whizzed in a liquidiser and served icy cold. In Sri Lanka a favourite drink is iced tea or coffee. Both are flavoured with vanilla or cardamom pods and sweetened with condensed milk. Chinese meals are best served with clear weak tea – flavoured with jasmine or orange flowers, lychee, passion fruit or mango. A pot of tea is placed on the table and frequently topped up with hot water.

One special recipe enjoyed in Sri Lanka, Indonesia and Malaysia is *Falooda* – a milk-based, rose water-flavoured drink with pieces of seaweed (*agar agar*) jelly, strands of cornflour vermicelli and *kasa-kasa*. This is a type of small seed (*tulsi* in Indian) which expands in water to form a jelly 'ball' surrounding a small crunchy middle. In Sri Lanka *kasa-kasa* is believed to lower body heat and is added to orange juice or barley water. In India, drinking *Lassi* is a good way to quench fiery hot curries. Whisk equal amounts of yoghurt and water together and either flavour with a little salt or, more acceptably, sugar and vanilla, rose or orange water or a pinch of ground cardamom, and serve with crushed ice.

MENUS

We have given some menu suggestions below. Sometimes it is better to serve one or two of the dishes first, as starters. We have indicated these with an asterisk(*).

Menu 1: SRI LANKAN (1)

Mulligatawny or Lentil Soup

Sri Lankan Hoppers (and Egg Hoppers)

and/or Coconut Rotis and Hodi

Coconut Sambol

Seeni Sambol

Mallung

Sri Lankan Lamb & Spinach Curry

Vattalapan

This menu has several interesting flavours, many of which will be new to readers. The Hodi (Coconut Soup) is poured on the Roti only enough to moisten it. The sambols and Vegetable Mallung really spice up the meal. Vattalapan is a delicious cardamom-flavoured custard served ice-cold.

Menu 2: SRI LANKAN (2)

* Onion Bhajiis

* Mint & Yoghurt Dip

Rasam

Biriyani

Salt Fish Curry and/or Beef Smoore

Pineapple Curry

Tomato, Cucumber & Onion Sambol

fresh green leaf salad

Avocado Ice Cream

Here the spicy Onion Bhajiis and Mint and Yoghurt Dip starter gives a taste of what is to come. The heat of the Biriyani, curries and Beef Smoore is balanced by the freshness of the Tomato, Cucumber and Onion Sambol. Sip the *Rasam* throughout the meal.

Avocado Cream is a beautiful green dessert, very rich and sumptuous but a lovely way to end a quite savoury meal.

Menu 3: CHINESE

Hot Sour Soup or Egg Drop Soup

Chicken Rice

cucumber batons

Cheena Patas Prawns and/or Beef Rendang

Stir-Fried Beans and/or Quick Fried Bean Sprouts

Sambol Ulek

Steamed Butter Cake with Ginger Cream

This meal displays hot flavours not usually associated with Chinese food. Hot Sour Soup is well named but if you want a tamer start to your meal try the better-known Egg Drop Soup instead. Chicken Rice is a meal in itself. Married with fiery Cheena Patas Prawns and vegetables and delicious dry Beef Rendang curry, followed by Butter Cake with Ginger Cream, this meal is easily prepared but tastes out of this world.

Menu 4: MALAYSIAN

Fried 'Seaweed'

Wontons

Satay and Sauce and/or Jewel Fish

Compressed Rice Cakes

Rasam

Turtle 'Eggs'

Starting with Fried Seaweed and finishing with a dessert called Turtle Eggs, this menu has a definite ocean theme! The *Rasam* adds an unexpected sharp note, which cuts through the richness of the fried dishes. Sip it throughout the meal to refresh the palate. This meal looks so lovely – with the deep green of the Seaweed, the browns and reds of the Satay and Sauce or the ravishing colours of Jewel Fish, then the pure white of the Rice Cakes. Textures are a key to this meal, too: crispy and crunchy, then smooth and creamy.

Menu 5: THAI

Tom Yum Kung

* Paper-wrapped Chicken and Mange Tout

* Quick Plum Sauce

Nam Prik

Char Sui Pork

Peking Pancakes

cucumber batons and shredded spring onion

Lo Mein (Noodles with Beef and Vegetables)

Tiger Lily Tamarind Fish (optional)

Almond Tea

What a sensational menu! Starting with Thailand's favourite soup and intriguing Paper Wrapped Chicken served with a sweet sauce, the happy eaters progress through dainty pancakes which they stuff at the table with cucumber and shredded spring onions, then cautiously dip in fiery *Nam Prik* (hot shrimp sauce) and Plum Sauce. Then come noodles and perhaps unusual spicy Tamarind Fish. The meal ends with icy clear sweetened water with creamy diamonds of almond-flavoured jelly. Great fun to eat and easy to cook – everything can be prepared in advance and finished off a few minutes before serving.

Menu 6: PARTY BUFFET

Chicken Batons

selection of dips and Gado Gado

Mixed Pakoras

Quick and Easy Naan Bread (make mini ones)

Shrimp Toasts

Bombay Mix

Tiger Lily Sweet & Sour Pork Ribs

Sweet and Sour Eggs

Marshmallows

Steamed Butter Cake

This menu will keep vegetarians and meat-eaters equally happy. Cut each Sweet and Sour Egg into 4 segments, the Shrimp Toasts into triangles and the Ribs into bite-sized pieces. We enjoy colour and texture in our food and this menu laid out on a crisp white banqueting cloth looks fabulous.

For 25 people use recipe quantities for 6–8, and make 4 times the recipe for the cake.

For 50 people use recipe quantities for 12–16 and make 8 cakes.

Storecupboard Ingredients & Essential Recipes

THERE ARE a few essentials you will need before you start using this book.

The essential tools are a pestle and mortar or electric coffee grinder, a liquidiser, some sharp knives and a wok or deep-fryer.

In the East our trusty pestle and mortar (usually made of stone) acts as a grinder, liquidiser and blender. We use it to pulverise ingredients such as whole spices, chillies, ginger and garlic. In the West, with the variety of machines available, we would suggest that whole spices are ground in a coffee grinder, sauces and liquids are achieved with a blender/liquidiser, food processors could be used for fine chopping and making pastes, while garlic could be crushed with a traditional garlic crusher. If a recipe requires minced ginger, an ordinary cheese grater does the job extremely well.

If you can afford it (and they are now very reasonably priced from catalogue stores like Index or Argos), we strongly advise you to invest in an electric rice boiler. The sheer bliss of automatic rice cooking will free you to experiment and banish forever grainy uncooked kernels or stodgy 'pudding-type' disasters.

STORECUPBOARD INGREDIENTS

The storecupboard ingredients are divided into two groups: essential items needed to concoct great-tasting meals; and optional extras, to make the recipes taste even more authentic.

Essential

ginger; garlic; soy sauce (we tend to use the darker variety as it is stronger); sugar (dark brown or white); salt; vinegar (we always use malt); oil (any vegetable oil or peanut or sunflower but *not* olive oil); black or white pepper; sherry (sweet or dry but we usually use sweet); fresh chillies (remove the seeds for less heat – we prefer to leave them in); ground chilli, coriander, cumin and turmeric; cinnamon sticks; cloves; sesame oil; coconut milk (powdered or in a tin); creamed coconut (in a block); onions; Heinz tomato ketchup; crunchy peanut butter; cornflour; chicken stock cubes (Knorr is best); ground mixed spice.

Optional

dried prawns; ginger wine; galangal; lemon grass; curry leaves; pandanus leaf (*rampe*); kaffir lime leaves; straw oyster mushrooms; dried tamarind (in a block); shrimp paste (*blachan*); fish sauce; jaggery (palm sugar); maldive fish; dried wood ear Chinese mushrooms; whole cardamom pods; *tung choi* (preserved Chinese vegetables).

When we give food workshops, we ask the audience to name some of the essential ingredients needed for Continental cooking – say Italian. Most will be able to reel off some or all of the following: garlic, onions, carrots, tomatoes, oregano, thyme, olive oil, bay leaves, parsley, basil and lemon juice.

However, when we ask them to say what they need to cook Oriental and South-East Asian meals they are rather vague. We will let you into a secret – if you can memorise some of the following list you will soon be turning out restaurant-quality meals at home. Start with garlic, ginger, coriander (the whole plant – leaves, stalk, root, and seeds ground to a powder), ground cumin and turmeric, lemon or lime juice and rind, lemon grass, galangal, oil (vegetable, peanut, or corn), onions, spring onions, soy sauce, brown sugar, cornflour, fish sauce, coconut cream or powder and, of course, chillies (whole and fresh, dried whole, crushed or in powder form). Those wishing for more authenticity should track down maldive fish, dried shrimps or prawns, *blachan* (shrimp paste), curry leaves, *rampe* (pandanus), sesame oil and kaffir lime leaves.

Generally the preparation is as follows: crush the garlic and ginger (or galangal), fry in hot oil, add the onions, then the meat, fish, chicken or vegetables, a selection of seasonings and some liquid. Simmer until the ingredients are cooked. If stir-frying, the minimum of liquid is added and the cooking is done over a fierce heat. These standard methods cover most recipes. The only 'finishing' for some dishes is the addition of coconut cream and lime or lemon juice. We always recommend that you serve little dishes of chilli sauce, *Balichaw* (p. 26) or Vietnamese Fish Sauce (p. 29) for those who like their food extra spicy.

We usually serve all the savoury dishes (including soups) at once on or in communal dishes. Guests help themselves to what they want and eat the dishes in whatever order they like. It is not against the rules to sip the soup in between mouthfuls of rice, curry, etc. Desserts are mostly a selection of the luscious fruits that grow so prolifically in our countries. When offering any of the cooked desserts, we find it best to do so in small amounts, as they are often very rich.

Ingredients vary in strength. For example, the smaller the chilli, the hotter the taste. Chilli powder also varies in its potency. Likewise fish sauce and even soy sauce can have quite different strengths. We have tried to keep the recipes in this book as standard as possible, and you should adjust the ingredients according to your own taste.

Incidentally, we debated whether to give authentic names for all these recipes but decided against it for two reasons. Firstly, because as we have added our own twist to several classical South-East Asian recipes, it would not be fair to claim that they are the original versions. And secondly, do you really want to know that Fried Rice Sticks (p. 90) is called *Phat Wun Sen* in Thailand? We promised you no mystique and no frills and so we have described most dishes by their contents to help you decide whether you will enjoy them or not.

Bon appétit!

ESSENTIAL RECIPES

The quick and easy way to really good Oriental and South-East Asian cooking is to make your own curry powders, pastes and sauces. Set aside a weekend to make a batch and keep the pastes and sauces in the refrigerator. Not only will you save the money you would have spent buying inferior products at inflated prices but you will have the satisfaction of making your own. Start with the Roasted Sri Lankan Curry Powder. The flavour is quite unique.

ROASTED SRI LANKAN CURRY POWDER

THIS IS A dark, intensely fragrant powder which is hot but also aromatic, and totally different to Indian curry powders. Sri Lanka (meaning 'resplendent island') has many names: Taprobane; Serendipity – the happy knack of finding something good while searching for something else (supposedly coined by Marco Polo when he stumbled across Sri Lanka while looking for India); Ceylon and the Spice Island. It gained this last name because nearly every known spice is grown there and it was once a centre of the spice trade.

Sri Lankan housewives have access to homegrown curry leaves, *rampe* (pandanus), lemon grass and pepper, and those fortunate enough to own land have clove and cinnamon trees and most of the other spices, too. In the past, homegrown and ground curry powders were the mark of the proud home-maker, although now modern mills produce very good mixes. We think Bolsts is about the best but it is still worth taking the initial trouble to make your own.

MAKES *around 1lb (450g)*

4oz (110g) coriander seeds
2oz (50g) cumin seeds
5oz (150g) dried red chillies
2oz (50g) fennel seeds
1 teaspoon fenugreek seeds
2 sticks of cinnamon, each about 2 inches (5cm) long
1 teaspoon cloves

1 teaspoon cardamom pods
2 tablespoons curry leaves
2 teaspoons black peppercorns
2 teaspoons mustard seeds
5 inches (12cm) *rampe* or pandanus (optional), chopped
2 tablespoons ground rice

1. Preheat the oven to 200°C/400°F/Gas Mark 6 and roast the spices for about 10 minutes.

2. Cool, then grind the whole spices in a blender or coffee grinder until smooth.

3. In a heavy-based frying pan, dry-roast the ground rice until it starts turning a light golden brown.

4. Add the rest of the ingredients and roast until the mixture becomes quite a dark brown. Keep stirring so as not to burn the spices.

5. When cool, store in an airtight container.

GARAM MASALA

THIS SPICE mix is sprinkled over cooked curries or added at the end of the cooking time. Use either ounces or grammes to measure the ingredients. Like all spices, garam masala should not be made or stored in large quantities. Fresh is best.

1 part coriander seeds

1 part black peppercorns

2 parts cumin seeds

2 parts cloves

4 parts cardamom pods or 2 parts
    cardamom seeds

1 part cinnamon sticks, broken into small
    pieces

1. Preheat the oven to 200°C/400°F/Gas Mark 6 and roast the spices for 10 minutes.

2. Cool, then place in a blender or coffee grinder and reduce to a fine powder. Do not use a food processor or it may damage the machine.

3. Sieve the powder and store in an airtight container.

THAI CURRY PASTES

THAI CUISINE relies on a combination of several flavours – hot chilli, sour, fishy (using strong dried prawn paste or lighter fish sauce), either clear or milky (using coconut milk), and often sweet. The essential ingredients are galangal (a type of aromatic ginger root) and lemon grass.

We have given recipes for a selection of pastes which can be made up and stored in the fridge. They are very hot so only use between 2 teaspoons and 2 tablespoons of each in 1lb (450g) ingredients – enough for a meal for 4–6 people.

Tastes vary so some of you will be diving in at the deep end and ladling it in. The potency of chillies also varies. Those not used to the searingly hot tastes of Sri Lanka and Thailand are advised to treat these recipes with caution and try 1 teaspoon at a time. All these pastes will last for at least a week in the refrigerator. Store in airtight containers.

Once you know how much you will use for each meal, you can do what we do and freeze individual portions in small plastic bags.

Each recipe should make enough paste for 2–4 meals for 4 people.

THAI RED CURRY PASTE 1

This curry paste is very hot and spicy. It is good in Thai soups and curries that are clear and do not use coconut milk.

4oz (110g) fresh red chillies, chopped
2oz (50g) chopped garlic
3 tablespoons chopped lemon grass
1 teaspoon chopped galangal or ginger

1 teaspoon chopped coriander root
1 tablespoon *blachan* (shrimp paste) or
  2 tablespoons dried shrimps
2 tablespoons oil

1. Grind all the ingredients together, preferably using a mortar and pestle, or using a blender.

2. Store in the fridge in an airtight container.

THAI RED CURRY PASTE 2

This paste is more aromatic and the addition of coconut makes it somewhat milder and creamier.

25 fresh red chillies, chopped

4 spring onions or 1 large onion, peeled and chopped

2 tablespoons vegetable oil

1 tablespoon chopped galangal or ginger

2 tablespoons fish sauce

1 teaspoon grated lime rind

½ teaspoon ground coriander

3 stalks of lemon grass, crushed

3 large cloves garlic, peeled and crushed

½ teaspoon caraway seeds

1oz (25g) coconut cream or 1oz (25g) powdered coconut milk

1. Combine all the ingredients and liquidise or process to a smooth paste in a food processor.

2. Store in an airtight bottle and refrigerate. It will last for at least a week.

THAI GREEN CURRY PASTE 1

The green of this curry paste comes from the fresh coriander leaves. Like all plant materials, the natural chlorophyll (green colour) oxidises in air, fading rapidly on picking and cooking. Although this paste will last for up to a week in the refrigerator, it should be used within 2 days for maximum impact, colour and flavour. It is best for the clear, hot, sour/sweet curries much beloved of the Thais.

15 green chillies, chopped

4 spring onions or 1 large onion, peeled and chopped

3 cloves garlic, peeled and roughly chopped

2 tablespoons oil

1 tablespoon chopped galangal or ginger

2 tablespoons fish sauce

1 tablespoon sugar

1 teaspoon *blachan* (shrimp paste) or 2 teaspoons dried shrimps

3 stalks of lemon grass, crushed

1 teaspoon ground coriander

4 tablespoons or 1 bunch of fresh coriander leaves, chopped

juice and grated rind of 2 limes

3 fresh kaffir lime leaves (optional)

Combine all the ingredients and liquidise or process to a smooth paste in a food processor.

THAI GREEN CURRY PASTE 2

This paste is creamier and more aromatic. Use in curries which include coconut milk.

4oz (110g) green chillies, chopped

1 tablespoon black peppercorns, ground

4 spring onions or 1 large onion, peeled
  and chopped

2 tablespoons chopped garlic

4 tablespoons chopped fresh coriander
  (including the root)

1 tablespoon grated lemon rind

2 tablespoons salt

1 tablespoon ground coriander

1 tablespoon ground turmeric

1 tablespoon ground cumin

3 stalks of lemon grass, crushed

1 tablespoon *blachan* (shrimp paste) or
  2 tablespoons dried shrimps

3 tablespoons oil

3oz (75g) block coconut cream, grated or
  3 tablespoons powdered coconut milk

Combine all the ingredients and liquidise or process to a smooth paste in a food processor.

OPPOSITE *Clockwise from top:* Tiger Lily Sweet and Sour Sauce (page 30), toasted sesame seeds, Chicken Batons (page 107), Fried Seaweed (48), Onion Bhajiis (40), Mint and Yoghurt Dip (page 42)

OPPOSITE PAGE 25 *Clockwise from top:* Satay Sauce (page 32), Gado Gado (page 142), Tiger Lily Tamarind Fish (page 120)

SRI LANKAN CURRY SAUCE

WE WOULD normally blanch at the thought of a curry sauce. However, there is no denying that it makes a busy person's life much easier. We concocted this sauce especially for our regular customers at Alexandra Palace food shows who begged us to come up with a convenient way of making curry. We advise you to freeze it in quantities to suit your own needs. A quarter of this amount is sufficient for approximately 1lb (450g) ingredients. This sauce is used in several recipes in the book, such as Sri Lankan Lamb and Spinach Curry (page 103). To use it in your own curry recipes, simply brown the meat, fish or other main ingredients of your choice then add the curry sauce, bring to the boil then lower the heat and simmer for about 15 minutes until the curry thickens, stirring constantly.

MAKES *about 8fl oz (225ml) sauce or 16 portions*

4 cloves garlic, peeled and roughly chopped

5 inch (12cm) piece of ginger, peeled and roughly chopped

2 medium onions, peeled and roughly chopped

14fl oz (400ml) water

2 × 14oz (400g) tins tomatoes

2 tablespoons oil (preferably coconut oil)

2 teaspoons dried maldive fish or dried shrimps, grated or powdered (optional)

1 tablespoon Roasted Sri Lankan Curry Powder (p. 20)

3 teaspoons ground turmeric

4 teaspoons salt

6 curry leaves (optional)

1 × 7oz (200g) block coconut cream

1. Put the garlic, ginger, onions, and a little of the water in a blender or food processor and process until creamy. Keep to one side.

2. Liquidise the tomatoes in the same blender. Keep to one side.

3. Heat the oil in a pan and add the garlic cream. Keep stirring until all the water evaporates and the mixture begins to brown.

4. Add the maldive fish or dried shrimps, curry powder, turmeric, salt and curry leaves, if using. Stir until the mixture begins to form a paste and the oil begins to separate.

5. Add the coconut cream, tomatoes and the rest of the water, covering the pan to prevent spitting. Bring to the boil, then simmer for 15–20 minutes. Tinned tomatoes vary in the amount of liquid they contain. Your sauce should be thick and fragrant. Taste and add extra salt if necessary.

6. Freeze in 4 separate bags/containers or in ice cube trays for easy-to-use individual blocks.

BALICHAW
DRY SHRIMP APPETISER

THIS POPULAR Burmese sambol will keep for up to a month in the refrigerator, stored in a clean dry glass jar with an airtight screw-on lid. An excellent standby to pep up curries and stir-fries alike, *Balichaw* is also delicious sprinkled onto soup. Try adding a small teaspoonful to omelettes, or in a baked potato.

SERVES 4–6

2–3 tablespoons vegetable oil

1 medium onion, peeled and thinly sliced

5 cloves garlic, peeled and thinly sliced

2oz (50g) dried shrimps

½ teaspoon *blachan* (shrimp paste)

2 tablespoons malt vinegar

1 teaspoon salt

1 teaspoon chilli powder

1. Heat 2 tablespoons oil in a frying pan and add the onion and garlic. Fry over a high heat until golden brown and crispy, stirring all the time. Add extra oil if necessary.

2. Remove the onions and garlic from the oil with a slotted spoon and dry on kitchen paper.

3. Add the dried shrimps to the oil in the frying pan and fry for at least 3 minutes, stirring all the time until they turn crispy too.

4. Mash the shrimp paste with the vinegar, salt and chilli powder and add to the pan.

5. Stir the contents of the pan over a medium heat until the mixture becomes dry. Remove from the heat, and add the onions and garlic.

6. Cool, then store in the fridge for up to a month.

NAM PRIK

HOT SHRIMP SAUCE

DYNAMITE! This hot mix is much loved by Thais who use it as a dipping sauce with fresh-cut raw vegetables and small batons of fried fish, cold meat and chicken. It's very good with Char Sui Pork (p. 98) too. There are as many variations of *Nam Prik* as there are cooks in Thailand. This is the one used by our servants and cherished by some of our bosom friends. Unfortunately, *Nam Prik* breath, which lasts until the next day, is a fearsome thing. You have been warned but, believe us, the amazing taste is well worth the anti-social penalty.

SERVES 4

1 tablespoon dried shrimps
2 teaspoons *blachan* (shrimp paste)
3 cloves garlic, peeled
3 slices ginger, peeled
1½ tablespoons lemon juice
1 tablespoon soy sauce

2–3 tablespoons jaggery (palm sugar) or
   brown sugar
1oz (25g) fresh red chillies, chopped
1 teaspoon water
1 teaspoon salt

1. Soak the dried shrimps in water for 15 minutes, then rinse and drain.

2. Wrap the *blachan* in a little foil, and grill for 1 minute on each side.

3. Pound the garlic and ginger and shrimps together, then add the *blachan* and finally the rest of the ingredients. Alternatively, put the whole lot in a blender and whizz for a few minutes.

4. Serve with great caution but bliss!

SAMBOL ULEK
INDONESIAN CHILLI PASTE

THIS IS scorchingly hot so eat it in very small quantities! *Sambol Ulek* is wonderful stirred into other dishes to add just that extra bit of fire. Keep it in an airtight jar in the refrigerator and it will last for several weeks.

SERVES 4

20 fresh red chillies
1 teaspoon salt

5fl oz (150ml) malt vinegar

1. Liquidise the ingredients until smooth.

2. Use with immense caution as a relish.

VARIATION
✦ The Thais have their own version of this using 8 red chillies and 6 tablespoons lime juice. This will keep for up to a week in the refrigerator.

VIETNAMESE FISH SAUCE

Lovely to use as a dipping sauce for Stuffed Spring Rolls (p. 50) or just to spice up any dish instead of ordinary soy sauce. This sauce is only faintly fishy – more sweet, sour and hot – and quite delicate, even with the garlic.

SERVES 4–6

8 tablespoons fish sauce
2 garlic cloves, peeled and crushed
juice and flesh of 2 lemons

2 fresh red chillies
1 tablespoon sugar

1. Put all the ingredients into a liquidiser with 4 tablespoons water and blend for a few minutes.

2. Serve in small bowls.

TIGER LILY'S SPECIAL SWEET & SOUR SAUCE

THIS SAUCE is perfect for dipping or pouring over small pieces of meat, fish, etc, deep-fried in a crisp batter.

4fl oz (110ml) tomato ketchup (preferably Heinz)

1 tablespoon malt vinegar

3 tablespoons sugar

2 cloves garlic, peeled and crushed

1 teaspoon fresh minced ginger

1 tablespoon crushed pineapple (tinned in syrup is fine)

1 tablespoon cornflour, blended with 3 tablespoons water

1. Combine all the ingredients in a saucepan except for the cornflour mixture, add 4fl oz (110ml) water and bring to the boil.

2. Add the cornflour and bring to the boil again, stirring until the mixture thickens.

VARIATIONS

✦ Try adding slices of sweet peppers, onions and carrots. Blanch any combination of these in boiling water, refresh immediately under a cold tap, and add to the hot sauce. Cook for a few minutes to let the flavours sink in but not long enough to make the vegetables limp and flabby.

✦ If liked, stir in some roasted cashew nuts and chunks of pineapple before serving.

✦ To make the sauce spicy, add ½–1 teaspoon chilli powder, and/or 1 teaspoon Worcestershire sauce.

QUICK PLUM SAUCE

I F YOU have run out of hoi sin or plum sauce, the shops are closed and your Peking duck and pancakes are ready to serve, you can always whip up a batch of this super-easy alternative. It is equally good as a dipping sauce for Wontons (p. 46) or Stuffed Spring Rolls (p. 50).

MAKES *about 5fl oz (150ml) sauce*

4fl oz (110ml) plum or peach jam (look for the one with the highest fruit content)
1fl oz (25ml) chutney

2 tablespoons malt vinegar
½ teaspoon chilli powder (optional)

Place all the ingredients in a liquidiser and blend until smooth.

Satay sauce

A N ESSENTIAL sauce to accompany Satay (p. 95) or the Indonesian vegetable salad, Gado Gado (p. 142).

This recipe evolved from our desire to use what was freely available and cut down on time and effort but not at the expense of taste. We would use fresh peanuts and grind them ourselves back home, but long live crunchy peanut butter from the supermarket!

When serving this sauce, remember to warn your guests that it contains peanuts in case anyone suffers from an allergic reaction.

SERVES 6–8

1 small onion, peeled and very finely
  chopped
2 cloves garlic, peeled and crushed
2 fresh red chillies, chopped
3 tablespoons vegetable oil
2 teaspoons jaggery (palm sugar) or dark
  brown sugar
½ teaspoon salt
2 tablespoons soy sauce
1 tablespoon lime juice

1 stalk of lemon grass or grated rind of
  1 lemon
1 teaspoon *blachan* (shrimp paste),
  wrapped in foil and grilled for 1 minute
  on each side (optional)
4oz (110g) creamed coconut block mixed
  with 15fl oz (425ml) hot water
1lb (450g) crunchy peanut butter
½ teaspoon chilli powder (optional)

1. Fry the onion, garlic and chillies in the oil until they begin to brown.

2. Add all the remaining ingredients except for the coconut cream and peanut butter, bring to the boil and simmer for 5 minutes.

3. Stir in the coconut cream and peanut butter and simmer until the sauce thickens and the oil just begins to separate.

4. Taste and adjust the seasoning, adding ½ teaspoon chilli powder and more salt if liked. If the sauce is too thick, add a little extra hot water to thin it down.

HOMEMADE CHICKEN STOCK

EVERY CHINESE cook will have a store of this stock in his or her refrigerator. If you remember to give it a good boil (at least 5 minutes on a high rolling boil) once a week, cool, then refrigerate it, the stock will last up to 3 weeks. Most of our Chinese recipes call for anything from a tablespoon to several pints of this stock, so it is worth making your own if you have the time and the inclination. Alternatively, you could use Knorr chicken stock cubes which are very authentic and almost as good.

1 × 4lb (1.8kg) boiling fowl or same weight   1 tablespoon salt
   in chicken wings (this is a good way to
   use those wing tips discarded when you
   make Chicken Batons, p. 108)

1. Clean the chicken, removing any yellow fat from the body cavity. Save this, melt it and use for stir-fries or for cooking fabulous golden roast potatoes. Chicken fat (like all animal fats) is high in cholesterol but the taste is superb and you will not be eating enough to cause any permanent damage to your arteries.

2. Put the chicken into a very large pan with the salt, add 9 pints (5 litres) water, and bring to the boil. Simmer for up to 3 hours or cook in a pressure cooker for 30 minutes.

3. Cool, strain and store in an airtight container in the refrigerator. Alternatively, pour into ice-making trays, and freeze into cubes. When you need it, just pop a frozen cube into your dish. What could be simpler? Save the chicken meat for chicken rillettes – remove some of the skin and discard. Then use 2 forks to shred the flesh (and some skin), add salt and pepper, mix with a little melted butter and eat on toast. Simply delicious.

VARIATION

✦ The Chinese love pork as much as chicken, so you may want to use pork bones instead of chicken. Remember to remove the fat which will harden on the surface when the stock cools. You are after a clear, well-flavoured stock.

SAMBOLS

IT IS interesting to compare dishes from around the world. For instance, South American salsas – raw tomato, onion and chillies whizzed together in a food processor and brought to life with lemon juice and salt – give the taste buds a touch of excitement, just like Eastern sambols. Every meal in Sri Lanka is served with at least one sambol on the side. These can be enhanced by the more Western accompaniment of green salad leaves, adding freshness, colour, texture and vitamins to enliven the meal.

COCONUT SAMBOL

This is definitely our bestselling instant mix and one that Michelin-starred chef Bruno Loubet (of L'Odéon, Piccadilly), Cyrus Todiwala (of Café Spice Namaste of the City) and Henry Harris (of Harvey Nichols' The Fifth Floor Restaurant) use in many of their own recipes.

As an island, Sri Lanka is surrounded by swaying rustling coconut palms and we make use of all its products. Its leaves are woven into mats and shelters; its nuts provide coconut flesh, milk and oil; the husk gives *copra* to fill mattresses and provide gardening centres across the world with eco-friendly compost; its trunk is used for wood, carvings, furniture and kindling. From birth, Sri Lankans use coconut oil to keep their skins soft and wrinkle-free and on their hair to ensure it remains shiny and dark. Oh yes, and its juice can be fermented to produce a mind-blowing native moonshine called toddy.

You will find references to Coconut Sambol throughout this book. Not only can it be served with Rice (p. 67), Hoppers (p. 74), Mock Stringhoppers (p. 88) and Coconut Rotis (p. 76), it can also be stirred into fried rice or noodles, added to soups or curries as a thickener, fried with cooked meat, onions and potatoes for an instant spicy dry curry, and even added to pancake mixture, baked potatoes or cheese on toast.

Eat it often but in modest amounts – it should be quite spicy.

SERVES 4

4oz (110g) fresh or desiccated coconut
1 teaspoon salt
1 teaspoon chilli powder
2 teaspoons maldive fish or ground dried
   shrimps
3 curry leaves

1 small piece *rampe* (pandanus),
   approximately 1 inch (2.5cm) long
1 medium onion, peeled and roughly
   chopped
1 teaspoon lemon juice

1. Mix 2 tablespoons boiling water into the coconut to moisten. If using desiccated coconut add a further 2 tablespoons hot water.

2. Put the rest of the ingredients into a liquidiser and whizz for a few seconds only. It should not become a paste.

3. Combine all the ingredients and serve with just about anything, at any time! Coconut sambol will last up to 3 days in a refrigerator or can be frozen for up to 2 months. Freeze in small amounts, enough for one meal.

How to use fresh coconut – if you really must!

1. Select a fresh-looking nut and shake it. You should be able to hear some water sloshing around. This is not the milk – you make that by squeezing the grated coconut flesh in hot water and straining it.

2. Hold the nut in the palm of your hand with the 3 'eyes' at the top. Use the blunt edge of a large cleaver (not the sharp blade) to tap gently all the way around its centre. Imagine it is the world and you are creating the equator!

3. Sharply tap the nut with the knife. With practice, it should divide neatly into 2 halves.

4. In Sri Lanka, someone would grate the coconut using a fearsome implement similar to a giant serrated screwdriver with 5 heads. You can cheat by cutting off the thin brown skin and putting the white flesh into your food processor on fast speed for only a few seconds.

5. We strongly suggest you forget this and go for your storecupboard packet of desiccated coconut!

TOMATO, CUCUMBER & ONION SAMBOL

One very strange thing we noticed when we returned east after many years of living in the West, was the absence of the green ridged cucumbers we were so used to seeing and eating. Now we were faced with huge barrage balloon-sized yellow cucumbers. We were told that, even if seeds from the green ones were planted, after a season or two they would mutate into the yellow ones. We never stayed long enough in one place to test this out but it sounds plausible. Another odd feature of the yellow cucumbers was that you had to cut a slice off the end, wait until it oozed a little milky sap and rub this vigorously across the cut end. If you forgot, the whole cucumber would taste bitter. The skin was very coarse so it had to be removed.

For this recipe try to get the tastiest possible tomatoes and onions. Turn resolutely away from the perfect but tasteless red salad tomatoes and select their misshapen but deliciously sweet and juicy Spanish cousins, or better still grow your own.

SERVES 4–6

1lb (450g) tomatoes
½ cucumber
1 medium onion, peeled and finely
   chopped
1 teaspoon salt

½ teaspoon sugar
2 teaspoons malt vinegar, or lemon or lime
   juice
1 teaspoon chilli powder

1. Dice the tomatoes and cucumber and add to the rest of the ingredients.

2. Mix and serve, preferably in a glass dish.

3. This sambol can be prepared up to 5 hours in advance but it must be eaten on the same day.

VARIATION

◆ The addition of a little Coconut Sambol (p. 34) will give this dish an extra zip.

SEENI SAMBOL
SUGAR SAMBOL

This is the other indispensable item on every Sri Lankan table. *Seeni Sambol* can be eaten with bread, Hoppers (p. 74), Mock Stringhoppers (p. 88), Rice (p. 67) ... the list is endless. It is the 'Siamese twin' of our beloved Coconut Sambol (p. 34) so do try it. This sambol will keep for up to 3 days in the refrigerator but rarely lasts that long because it is so 'more-ish'. Even if cooking a meal for 4, do make up this quantity and keep the balance.

SERVES 8

9fl oz (250ml) coconut or vegetable oil (but not olive oil)
1lb (450g) onions, peeled and finely sliced
4oz (110g) maldive fish or dried shrimps, pounded
1½ tablespoons chilli powder
2 teaspoons salt
8 curry leaves

2 tablespoons malt vinegar
a 2 inch (5cm) piece of cinnamon stick
a small piece of ginger, peeled and crushed
1 teaspoon ground mixed spice or allspice
1 dessertspoon coconut powder or a small 2 inch (5cm) cube from a block of coconut cream
1 tablespoon sugar

1. Heat the oil in a heavy frying pan and cook the onions slowly, stirring occasionally, until they turn transparent and all the water evaporates. This can take 15–20 minutes.

2. When the onions begin to caramelise and turn a delicious golden brown (the smell is absolutely mouthwatering), add the rest of the ingredients except for the sugar, and simmer for 5–10 minutes.

3. Keep stirring until all the liquid has evaporated and the oil starts to separate and rise to the top. Stir in the sugar.

4. Taste and adjust the seasoning, adding more salt and chilli powder if liked. The sambol should be hot, sweet and savoury.

TAMARIND CHUTNEY

A SPICY, sweet and sour chutney that has a very unusual fruity flavour. We love this with cheese and French bread as well as with our rice and curries.

MAKES *about 2¾ lb (1.25kg) chutney or 5 jars*

1lb (450g) tamarind block
8oz (225g) chopped stoned dates
4oz (110g) sultanas
1 tablespoon chilli powder
1 teaspoon ground cinnamon
4 cloves garlic, peeled and chopped

a 1 inch (2.5cm) piece of ginger, peeled
  and crushed
3fl oz (75ml) malt vinegar
2 teaspoons salt
4oz (110g) jaggery (palm sugar) or dark
  brown sugar

1. Soak the tamarind in hot water for about 15 minutes until soft. Mash the pulp and strain, keeping only the liquid.

2. Combine all the ingredients in a pan and cook over a low heat, stirring continuously, until the mixture has the consistency of jam.

3. Bottle in clean dry jars. This fruity chutney will keep for 6 months

Starters

THIS CHAPTER is a collection of our favourite recipes which mirrors our diverse background. Wontons (p. 46), Prawn Toasts (p. 49), Fried 'Seaweed' (p. 51) and Stuffed Spring Rolls (p. 50) come from our Chinese heritage and the others our Asian roots. South-East Asians and Orientals, like the Sri Lankans, do not have traditional starters. Instead, all the dishes are placed together on the table at once and it is customary to help yourself to a little of everything. You will find many recipes elsewhere in the book that would also make ideal starters, if you feel the need to divide your meal into Western-style courses.

We have given you this choice of raitas, dips, *Chavada* (p. 52) and our beloved Onion Bhajii recipe (p. 40) for no other reason than that we love them! A good way to serve the dips is with small baskets filled with some or all of the following to scoop the lovely flavours up:

- prawn crackers
- tortilla chips or crisps
- mini poppadoms or large ones carefully cut into strips before frying (they are far too delicate to cut after they are cooked)
- raw vegetables, like celery, cucumber, tomatoes, lettuce leaves
- strips of cooked meat or fish, dipped in a simple batter and deep-fried

- French bread, Quick and Easy Naan Bread (p. 82), Roll Dough (p. 74) all made mini-sized or cut into manageable pieces

These make interesting cocktail or buffet finger food.

If you really must serve the dips as a starter, try cutting up a portion of Indonesian Grilled Spicy Chicken (p. 113), nestle the chicken pieces on a bed of shredded lettuce and serve instead of the usual tandoori chicken.

ONION BHAJIIS

THIS WAS one of the very first recipes we tailor-made for Harvey Nichols. We used to handwrite the labels and stick them on plastic sandwich bags of instant mix, then felt very grand when we went upmarket and had the labels photocopied! After 12 months cautiously surveying the soaring sales figures we realised we had a winner and leapt into ordering printed bags with the recipe on them – 20,000 at a time – and included them in our first mail-order list.

Whenever we are asked by friends to bring some nibbles along for parties these are always the first to disappear.

Chickpea (also known as besan, gram or channa) flour is a dream to use. Gluten-free, it sticks like concrete to raw meat, fish, etc, and, unlike breadcrumbs, doesn't have the annoying habit of falling off food when you fry it. It mixes with water to make a lump-free cream which is then flavoured with spices.

Although the recipe below is for Onion Bhajiis, any partly cooked vegetable can be added, e.g. peas, potatoes, cauliflower florets or whole baby mushrooms. Strips of meat (partly cooked in a microwave or steamed for a few minutes) can also be used, such as chicken, beef, fish, etc. They are then called *pakoras*.

Bhajiis and *pakoras* freeze well (up to 2 months). Defrost and heat for a short time in a microwave or oven when needed. They are particularly useful if you want to prepare party food in advance.

If you can't find besan flour anywhere, you can substitute pea flour from a healthfood shop, or make your own. Dry-roast 1lb (450g) chickpeas or yellow split peas in a heavy pan on top of the stove over a medium heat. Stir the peas constantly with a wooden spoon to prevent them burning. When lightly toasted, cool then put the peas through an electric coffee grinder or blender on high speed until powdered. Sift, then store in an airtight container.

MAKES *up to 50 small cocktail-sized* bhajiis *or 25 larger ones*
SERVES *4–6 for a meal or 20 as part of a buffet*

8oz (225g) chickpea flour
1 dessertspoon each of ground cumin, coriander and salt
1 teaspoon each of ground black pepper, turmeric, and chilli powder

2 large onions, peeled and chopped, or 1lb (450g) alternative ingredients suggested above (eg. peas, potatoes etc.)
2 pints (1 litre) oil for deep-frying

1. Sieve the flour into a deep bowl, add the dry ingredients and 7fl oz (200ml) water and mix vigorously with a wooden spoon until it becomes a smooth cream.

2. Add the onions, or alternative ingredients, and ensure they are well coated in batter.

3. Heat the oil in a wok or deep-fryer until it begins to smoke. A drop of batter will immediately rise to the surface and begin to turn brown when the oil is at the right temperature. Turn the temperature down to medium heat.

4. Use either 2 teaspoons for cocktail-sized *bhajiis*, or 2 dessertspoons for larger ones, and scoop spoonfuls of batter into the oil. Use the second spoon to push it off the first so you get a uniform shape and size.

5. Fry a few at a time, turning them once. When they begin to turn brown, take them out with a slotted spoon and drain on crumpled paper towels.

6. Serve with a range of chutneys and yoghurt dips.

VARIATION

♦ For an even more special taste, add 1 tablespoon finely chopped fresh coriander leaves and/or 1 teaspoon mint sauce to the batter before adding the onions, etc.

SPECIAL DIPS

EVERYONE's heart sinks when confronted by the obligatory tray of sad-looking cucumber, celery and carrot sticks, usually served with some violent pink taramasalata and grey hummus, which pass for crudités or hors d'oeuvres at cocktail parties. Strange how this always seems to be the one tray that remains virtually untouched throughout, and ends up being swept into the bin.

Instead, try batons of raw courgettes or turnip (use young ones that have not gone spongy), whole cherry tomatoes, boiled quail's eggs, and lightly steamed sticks of beetroot, mange tout or small French beans.

Slices of fresh peeled fruit, such as mangoes, peaches, nectarines or pears, can also add a stunning visual contrast and interesting flavour but remember to go for freshness, crunch and colour. Add some Onion Bhajiis (p. 40), poppadoms and mini pitta breads or Coconut Rotis (p. 76) and you have a substantial starter. Served with a Lentil Soup (p. 54) and bread, it becomes a balanced meal, just bursting with vitamins and taste.

So walk resolutely past the cold larder selection of supermarket 'dips' and try making your own.

MINT & YOGHURT DIP

This dip is so simple we are almost embarrassed to include it. But it tastes so good and is as much at home partnered with Indonesian Grilled Spicy Chicken (p. 113) as Onion Bhajiis (p. 40) and poppadoms so we just had to share it with you. It is also very pretty – golden yellow with flecks of bright green. Strangely enough, the cheapest, most sugary and vinegary supermarket brand mint sauce is the best for this recipe.

SERVES 4

10fl oz (275ml) plain yoghurt (preferably the thick set Greek type)	¼ teaspoon each of chilli powder, ground coriander and cumin
2 teaspoons ground turmeric	1 dessertspoon mint sauce
½ level teaspoon salt	sugar, to taste

1. Drain off any liquid from the yoghurt, then place in a bowl and beat with a fork until smooth.

2. Add the remaining ingredients and blend well.

3. Serve in a pretty shallow bowl. If you are delicate by nature, and steady of hand, you can decorate the top of the bowl with concentric circles made from pinches of turmeric, cumin, coriander and paprika. It does look wonderful!

TAMARIND & DATE DIP

This is one of the easiest yet most scrumptious dips we have had the good fortune to encounter. Deep brown, hot and spicy but deliciously sweet and sour too.

We had an aunt with a tamarind tree in her garden and we just couldn't wait for the season to come round when we could gorge ourselves on the long papery pods with their deliciously sticky centres and dark shiny seeds, even though we usually suffered from tummy ache afterwards. Many animals shared our love of the fruit, and fruit bats, monkeys and even elephants were occasionally sighted around the heavily laden tree.

Tamarind is used in the East as a preservative instead of vinegar and lemon juice. Its tart, sweet yet sour flavour is unsurpassed in curries and soups. Buy it in dark dried blocks of 8oz (225g) or 1lb (450g) weight. This dip is especially good with seafood or with traditional Peking Pancakes (p. 84) and roast duck.

SERVES 6

8oz (225g) dried tamarind (seedless if possible)	1 teaspoon each of salt, ground cumin and coriander
8oz (225g) stoned dates, chopped	1–2 teaspoons chilli powder
juice of 2 limes or 1 tablespoon lemon juice	a few sesame seeds (optional)

water, pour over the tamarind and soak for 30 minutes.

2. Strain through a sieve to remove the seeds (if any) and pith. Some tamarind blocks are more fibrous than others – don't be afraid to squeeze the pulp with well-washed hands like we do in the Orient.

3. Mix the strained liquid with all the other ingredients except the sesame seeds, put in a saucepan and simmer, uncovered, for about 15 minutes.

4. Cool, then sieve again and liquidise. Place the thick sauce in a bowl and serve. If the sauce is too thick, add a little hot water to thin it down.

5. Sprinkle the sesame seeds on top of the dip, for contrast, if you wish.

COCONUT, CORIANDER & CHILLI DIP

A beautiful pale green dip or sauce that will add colour to your buffet table. It's excellent with *pakoras* (p. 40) and Chicken Batons (p. 108).

SERVES 4–6

8oz (225g) desiccated coconut
1oz (25g) chopped fresh coriander
4 fresh green chillies

1–2 teaspoons salt
1 tablespoon each of sugar and lemon juice

1. Put all the ingredients in a blender or food processor with 4fl oz (110ml) water and process until smooth. Leave to stand for an hour for the flavours to develop.

2. Serve in a shallow bowl, or use a halved melon (remove some of the flesh and all of the seeds) as a container and scatter a few edible flower petals on top. Try nasturtiums or marigolds.

TOMATO, GARLIC & CHILLI DIP

This spicy, sweet tomato dip with undertones of garlic is very good with strips of chicken or fish dipped in batter and fried, or with freshly boiled shrimps or prawns.

Heinz could have stopped at baked beans and tomato ketchup for all we care, and forgotten about the other 55 brands! We love both and would eat gallons of each, given half a chance. Heinz tomato ketchup is made with tomatoes, spices and little else, and is hard to beat as the tomato base for many of our sweet and sour recipes. If you can find an equal then use it by all means – but read the label carefully and please shun any that contain flour or thickeners. To our mind, the pastiness ruins the taste.

SERVES 4

4 tablespoons tomato ketchup
1 tablespoon malt vinegar
3 cloves garlic, peeled and very finely
   minced

1 teaspoon salt
2 teaspoons chilli powder

1. Put all the ingredients in a saucepan with 4 tablespoons water and simmer for 5–10 minutes.

2. Cool, then liquidise and serve in a shallow bowl. If you can get hold of a giant beef tomato, you can cut the top off, scoop out the inside and serve the dip in it.

Banana raita

EVERYONE must have eaten cucumber raita in an Indian restaurant. Mild, cooling and creamy, it helps to put out the fire of a too-hot curry. Why not try our fruit alternatives for a change? The sweetness is quite unusual. Do experiment with other fruit in season. Summer fruit could be equally pleasing – try adding raspberries, strawberries or even blackcurrants or elderberries.

SERVES 6–8

1 pint (570ml) thick set yoghurt
4 bananas, peeled, sliced and mixed with
  1 tablespoon lemon juice
2 green chillies, finely chopped

½ teaspoon ground coriander
½ teaspoon ground cumin
½ teaspoon salt

1. Drain off any liquid from the yoghurt, then place in a bowl and beat with a fork until smooth.

2. Add the remaining ingredients and blend well. Cover with cling film and refrigerate until needed. This dish does not keep well so it's best eaten the same day.

VARIATIONS

✦ Sprinkle 2 teaspoons chopped coriander leaves over as a garnish before serving.

✦ Replace the bananas with one of the following: 4oz (110g) pineapple, peaches or kiwi fruit, peeled, chopped and drained of juice.

WONTONS

WONTONS are Chinese ravioli which are boiled and served in soup or deep-fried and served with a range of dipping sauces. We know they are fattening when deep-fried and we should really steer clear of them but, oh, they are such a temptation . . .!

Wonton skins are little squares of egg and flour dough and they are readily available from Chinese speciality shops. If you cannot track them down, you can use filo pastry or make your own noodle dough and just roll it out very thinly before cutting it into 2 inch (5cm) squares or rounds. Your wontons may not look ultra-elegant but they will still taste wonderful.

The recipes for fillings on pages 47–48 will each make 25–40 wontons, enough to serve 6–8 people. You can use any of these recipes but do not over-fill your wontons or they will burst. This is how to fill them:

1. Put a very small amount of filling (about ½ teaspoon) in the middle of a square of dough. For folded wontons (see **a.** below), fold in half to make a triangle. Pinch the open sides together to seal, using a little water if necessary to make them stick. Fold the right and then the left corner up to the centre. Pinch together. For money-bag wontons (see **b.** below), bring all four corners together like a triangle. Dampen around the filling, with a little beaten egg, and press firmly to seal. There should be a frill of wonton pastry around the edge. Part of the pleasure of eating wontons is crunching through these frills.

2. Place the wontons on a lightly floured plate until ready to cook (see p. 48).

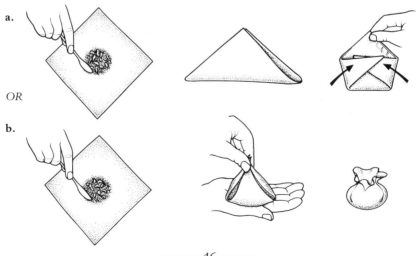

WHOLE PRAWN FILLING

Use uncooked raw prawns for the best results or else cooked cold water prawns with their shells on. Unfortunately 'cooking' or 'hot water' prawns will not do for this recipe as they just do not match the succulence and sweetness of their northern cousins.

1lb (450g) prawns or shrimps	salt and pepper

1. Peel the prawns, and remove the heads and black lines running down their backs (the intestinal tract).

2. Put a cleaned prawn in the centre of each wonton skin. Sprinkle with a little salt and pepper. Seal as described on p. 46.

PORK FILLING

Either use minced pork (make your own from any cut but discard any sinews and skin before chopping in a food processor, taking care not to over-process) or use best-quality pork sausage. If using the sausage make a slit down one side, remove the meat and throw away the skin. Choose a chunky cut sausage. You do not want a paste but a rough texture.

8oz (225g) minced pork or pork sausagemeat	½ teaspoon sweet sherry
½ teaspoon cornflour	½ teaspoon soy sauce
¼ teaspoon salt	2 tablespoons chopped canned water chestnuts

Mix all the ingredients together and use to fill wonton skins as described on p. 46).

CRAB & CHEESE FILLING

1 × 6oz (175g) tin crab meat or 6 crab sticks, finely chopped	¼ teaspoon ground black pepper
3oz (75g) cream cheese	2 spring onions, trimmed and finely chopped
½ teaspoon hoi sin sauce	

Mix all the ingredients together and use to fill wonton skins as described on p. 46.

VARIATION

✦ Try adding 2 tablespoons chopped watercress or 1 tablespoon very finely chopped celery. The first makes this filling delightfully peppery.

COOKING THE WONTONS

For fried wontons, deep-fry them in hot oil a few at a time. Remove with a slotted spoon when crispy and brown and drain on paper towels. Serve hot with Tiger Lily's Special Sweet and Sour Sauce (p. 30).

For boiled wontons, dissolve 2 good-quality chicken stock cubes in 1½ pints (900ml) water, or use the same quantity of Homemade Chicken Stock (p. 33). Bring to the boil and drop in the wontons. They are cooked when they float to the surface (about 5 minutes). Wash a bunch of watercress or a cup of shredded spinach or greens. Add to the soup. Bring to the boil for 2 minutes, and serve with soy sauce and a good chilli sauce.

Shrimp or prawn toasts

Pink 'cooking' prawns are not flavoursome but they come into their own in this dish. They are cheap and can be found lurking in the depths of most freezers. Your liquidiser will make quick work of them. We use left-over white supermarket bread which is going stale to make this impressive appetiser.

SERVES 6–8 *as a starter*

8oz (225g) peeled shrimps or prawns	2 tablespoons cornflour
1oz (25g) minced pork or meat from 1 good-quality pork sausage	12–15 slices thin cut white bread
1 tablespoon sherry	1 egg, lightly beaten
2 egg whites (size 3 or medium), beaten until stiff	1¾ pints (1 litre) oil for deep-frying

1. Place the shrimps or prawns, pork, sherry, egg whites, and half the cornflour in a liquidiser and blend to a thick paste.

2. Cut the bread into fingers or triangles, or stamp out into pretty shapes with cutters. Beat the left-over cornflour with the whole egg and brush the mixture over the pieces of bread.

3. Spread the shrimp paste over the bread shapes, then deep-fry in hot oil until golden, a few at a time, shrimp side down.

4. Turn after a few minutes and fry on the other side until golden.

5. Remove from the oil with a slotted spoon and drain on paper towels. Serve hot with Quick Plum Sauce (p. 31) or Tamarind and Date Dip (p. 43).

VARIATIONS

✦ Try adding a sprinkling of chopped coriander leaves and/or 1 finely chopped chilli before you spread the paste on the bread shapes.

✦ Crush 1 small clove of garlic and a little ginger together and add to the paste.

✦ 1 teaspoon sesame oil added to the paste, with a small amount of lime juice, gives it a Thai flavour.

✦ Sprinkle sesame seeds over the toast before frying, and press in lightly.

FRIED 'SEAWEED'

WE LOVE the crisp, almost cellophane texture of this dish, and its deep green colour. Using coarse-ground sea salt to season it brings back memories of the sea. Of course it isn't really seaweed – so don't be put off trying this surprisingly easy recipe. We serve it as a garnish for wontons with our Special Sweet and Sour Sauce (p. 30) for a really stunning starter.

Just take care not to burn the 'seaweed'. Cook it in very small batches, watch it like a hawk when it hits the hot oil and remove it as soon as it looks crisp. It will only take a few seconds. Take care to dry the leaves thoroughly on a tea towel before frying as any water will make the hot oil splatter.

SERVES 4

1lb (450g) spring greens or cauliflower leaves, washed and dried thoroughly	10fl oz (275ml) oil for deep-frying
	for sprinkling

1. Gather a few leaves together, roll into a cigar shape and, using a very sharp knife, cut into very thin shreds. Repeat with the other leaves.

2. Heat the oil in a wok or deep-fryer. When almost smoking add a handful of shreds and immediately begin to turn them with a slotted spoon.

3. Keep turning and moving around for a few seconds, then lift out and drain on paper towels. The 'seaweed' should be crisp and bright green in colour. Sprinkle with a little sea salt or ground dried prawns and serve.

STUFFED SPRING ROLLS

EITHER use bought wonton wrappers or make your own Peking Pancakes or Spring Roll Wrappers (p. 84). Everyone has a favourite recipe for these popular starters, but we love this one especially. This makes between 12 and 24 rolls, depending on the size. Tiny ones, the size of a baby's finger, are too enticing to be left alone, and well worth the initial effort.

Any left-over stir-fried dishes can be used up as spring roll fillings as long as they are not too liquid. You can thicken them by adding a little cornflour, then boiling if necessary. Taste and adjust the seasoning – the filling should be highly flavoured to contrast with the bland wrapper.

SERVES 4–6

1 × 7oz (200g) can bamboo shoots
1 medium carrot, peeled
2 sticks celery, washed and trimmed
1 teaspoon vegetable oil
1 clove garlic, peeled and crushed
3 spring onions, washed, trimmed and
   finely chopped (optional)
2oz (50g) bean sprouts

4oz (110g) shrimps or prawns, shelled and
   chopped
½ teaspoon sugar
½ teaspoon *Sambol Ulek* (p. 28)
1 teaspoon cornflour, mixed with
   1 teaspoon sherry
1 beaten egg
10fl oz (275ml) oil for deep-frying

1. Drain the bamboo shoots, then cut into very fine shreds. Cut the carrot and celery into thin strips.

2. Heat 1 teaspoon vegetable oil in a wok. When it begins to smoke add the garlic and vegetables and stir-fry for a few seconds only.

3. Lastly, add the shrimps or prawns, sugar, *Sambol Ulek* and cornflour mixture and stir for a few seconds more. Do not overcook, as the rolls will be fried again later. Put the filling aside to cool.

4. Take a wrapper, and place it on a floured surface. Cover the others so they do not dry out. Put about 2 teaspoons filling for the smaller rolls, and a tablespoon for the larger ones, at one end of each wrapper and fold the sides in. (See diagrams opposite.)

5. Brush the sides with beaten egg and roll firmly into cigar shapes. Take care to use plenty of egg and seal the ends properly.

6. Heat the oil in a wok or deep-fryer and cook the rolls until they are golden brown. Drain on paper towels and serve hot.

7. Sauces recommended to accompany this recipe are *Nam Prik* (p. 27), Tamarind and Date Dip (p. 43) or this special fish sauce: mix together 1 teaspoon *Sambol Ulek* (p. 28) with ½ teaspoon *Balichaw* (p. 26), 1 table-spoon fish sauce, 1 teaspoon sugar and 1 tablespoon malt vinegar.

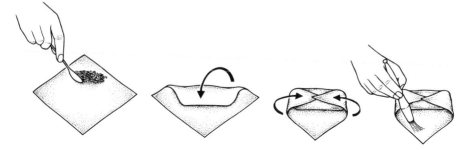

CHAVADA

BOMBAY MIX

WHY IS it that the most delicious things in life are always so bad for you? This applies to everything from men to marzipan, with fried foods somewhere in between!

Chavada is simple to prepare. It can be kept fresh for up to 5 weeks in an airtight container. This must be the only recipe we ask you *not* to make in bulk. Only because the temptation to have 'just a small handful' when passing it round will be too strong to resist and your waistline will not thank you (or us)!

SERVES 10–12

1lb (450g) dried *channa dhal* or chickpeas
1 pint (570ml) oil for deep-frying
8oz (225g) each of the following:
   rice crispies (yes, the kiddies' favourite
    breakfast cereal!)
   roasted salted peanuts
   crisps broken into smallish pieces

4oz (110g) sultanas (optional)
2 teaspoons salt
1 teaspoon ground turmeric
1 teaspoon chilli powder

1. Put the *channa* or chickpeas in a deep bowl and cover with at least 3½ pints (2 litres) water. Leave to soak overnight, after which they will have almost doubled in size.

2. Drain the chickpeas, then spread them out on a clean tea towel and allow to dry for about an hour.

3. Bring the oil up to smoking point in a wok or deep-fryer, lower the heat and fry small quantities of chickpeas until golden brown. Eat one – it should be crunchy but not too hard.

4. Lift the chickpeas out of the oil with a slotted spoon and allow to dry on paper towels.

5. Fry handfuls of the puffed rice in the same oil but watch carefully. They need only a few seconds and will burn quite easily if not taken out almost immediately. Dry on more paper towels.

6. Put all the ingredients into a bowl and mix thoroughly. Taste and adjust the seasoning, adding more chilli or salt if liked. Store in an airtight container.

VARIATION

✦ Add 8oz (225g) salted cashew nuts.

Soups

THIS CHAPTER includes a wide range of tastes and flavours, sweeping across South-East Asian cuisine like a giant paintbrush.

Hodi (p. 57) sits rather uncomfortably here, as it is not strictly a soup. It would never be served on its own but as a 'wetting agent' for dry dishes like Coconut Rotis (p. 76), Mock Stringhoppers (p. 88), or even plain Rice (p. 64). *Hodi* and *Rasam* (p. 59) can act as bases for unusual curries. *Hodi* creates mild 'white' curry while *Rasam*'s fiery, acidic taste peps up a hot curry. Simply slice vegetables or meat and boil or simmer them until tender in the chosen liquid, seasoning as required with extra chillies and other ingredients.

We include here everybody's favourites: like Mulligatawny (p. 58), beloved of ex-pats who still yearn for the days of the Raj; Thailand's hot *Tom Yum Kung* (p. 61) with its sharp mix of prawns, lemon grass and chillies; and China's ever-popular Egg Drop Soup (p. 60).

We have eaten in restaurants across the world and are sometimes disappointed, particularly in the suburbs, when cooks alter recipes supposedly to suit Western palates. This usually means cutting down on the seasoning, and bumping up the liquid, while overdosing on cornflour and the dreaded monosodium glutamate or 'tasty powder'.

If eating out, we always choose the ethnic quarter of any large city and are often to be found with our noses pressed up against steamy windows checking out the diners. If a Chinese restaurant is packed with Chinese that is our cue to enter and feast!

Tastes differ so we have tried to steer a middle course in our recipes – be generous with the extra seasoning if you like it that way, or add more water if you find the flavours too strong

LENTIL SOUP

❋

THIS deliciously creamy soup is not fiery hot, just pleasantly spicy. Do try it.

SERVES 6–8

6oz (175g) lentils (any type – we use the ordinary red ones most often)

3 carrots, peeled and chopped

3 large onions, peeled and chopped

1 stick celery, washed, trimmed and chopped

3 cloves garlic, peeled and crushed

2 teaspoons black peppercorns, freshly ground

1 teaspoon ground cumin

3 teaspoons salt

4 curry leaves (optional)

4oz (110g) coconut cream, cut into small cubes

2 teaspoons lime or lemon juice

1 teaspoon Garam Masala (p. 21)

1. Wash the lentils in several changes of water. Place in a large saucepan with all the ingredients except the coconut milk, lime or lemon juice and Garam Masala. Add 2½ pints (1½ litres) water, bring to the boil, then reduce the heat and simmer for 30 minutes or until all the vegetables are tender.

2. Put the soup through a liquidiser, return to the pan and add the coconut milk and lime or lemon juice. Stir in the Garam Masala, adjust the seasoning and serve with lots of hot crusty bread or with rice and curry.

VARIATION

✦ Try adding ¼ –½ teaspoon Thai Red or Green Curry Paste 2 (pp. 22–24) to the soup just before serving. Stir well.

CHINESE CHICKEN & MUSHROOM SOUP

I T MAKES us very happy that there are so many types of mushrooms flooding the market! Our favourites are fresh oyster, ordinary white 'buttons', tinned straw and dried wood ear. These last Chinese speciality mushrooms look like tiny brittle frills of black satin. Soak for 1–2 hours, then carefully strain off any impurities and use the mushrooms and their soaking water to add a delightful crunchy texture, rich flavour and colour contrast to any dish. They might seem expensive but you only use a few at a time and they seem to last forever.

SERVES 4–6

8oz (225g) raw chicken breast
2 pints (1¼ litres) Homemade Chicken Stock (p. 33), or 2 good-quality chicken stock cubes dissolved in the same quantity of water
4oz (110g) mixed mushrooms, drained if canned, sliced or quartered depending on size and shape (some supermarkets have started stocking a mixed variety – use this for convenience)
½ teaspoon ground white pepper
½ teaspoon sugar
2 spring onions, washed, trimmed and chopped

1. Slice the chicken breast into long, thin slivers with a very sharp knife and set aside.

2. Put the chicken stock into a saucepan and bring to the boil.

3. Add the mushrooms and boil for only 3 minutes. Then add the chicken, pepper and sugar and boil for another 3 minutes or until the meat turns opaque. Do not over-cook.

4. Scatter the chopped spring onions over the soup and serve.

VARIATIONS

✦ Stir 1 teaspoon sesame oil into the finished soup.

✦ If a spicier taste is desired, try adding any one of our Thai Curry Pastes (pp. 22–24) but in very small quantities (only ⅛ teaspoon). This soup is meant to be delicate.

HOT SOUR SOUP

Aₙ UNIQUELY tangy soup. We took Justin's (Rani's eldest son's) girlfriend Caroline out for one of our innumerable family dinners in Soho. It was the first time she had met us en masse and, being the exquisitely polite girl she is, she ate a little of everything rather than offend. Justin had ordered his favourite, fiery Hot Sour Soup – Caroline is very fair and turned nearly puce when she tried it!

Tofu, or bean curd, is found in many shops now. Very nutritious, it is delicate and needs gentle handling. Strain off the water it is stored in, then cut into cubes. Tofu can also be deep-fried and drained on paper towels. It has no taste on its own, but soaks up the flavour of whatever it is added to.

SERVES 4

1 pint (570ml) Homemade Chicken Stock (p. 33) or 1 chicken stock cube dissolved in the same quantity of water

2 tablespoons malt vinegar

½ teaspoon salt

½ teaspoon ground white pepper

1 teaspoon Thai Green Curry Paste 1 (p. 23)

3 tablespoons cornflour, mixed to a cream with 3 tablespoons water

4oz (110g) cooked sliced chicken

2oz (50g) each of sliced canned bamboo shoots, water chestnuts, and dried wood ear mushrooms, soaked and sliced (add liquid to the soup)

2oz (50g) tofu, cut into small cubes about the size of a thumbnail

2oz (50g) frozen garden peas

1 tablespoon soy sauce

1. Put the chicken stock, vinegar, salt, pepper and curry paste into a saucepan and bring to the boil.

2. Add the cornflour mixture and stir until it begins to thicken. Lower the heat, add the rest of the ingredients and heat through. Take care not to break up the cubes of tofu when serving.

VARIATION

✦ If liked, a teaspoon each of sherry and sesame seed oil can be added before serving.

OPPOSITE *Clockwise from top:* Seeni Sambol (page 37), Coconut Sambol (page 34), Sri Lankan Lamb and Spinach Curry (page 120), Yellow Rice (page 66)

Hodi

Coconut Milk Soup

ALTHOUGH not strictly a soup, this Sri Lankan speciality is made by every household almost daily. It is usually poured over stringhoppers (p. 88), steamed lacy pancakes made of rice flour, or *pittu* – a savoury made with fresh coconut, and flour, steamed in a hollow bamboo and sliced to eat with curry.

We had to improvise when we arrived in the West and found that many of the foods we loved were no longer available. This is a simplified recipe we devised. Do not boil; warm it gently or it will curdle.

A variety of vegetables, shellfish and even diced meat can be included to make a mild 'white' curry. You can add heat if you wish with a teaspoon of Thai Red or Green Curry Paste 2 (p. 22–24) or Balichaw (p. 26).

Although the optional ingredients add the truly authentic flavour, the soup tastes just as good without them.

SERVES 4

1 pint (570ml) Homemade Chicken Stock (p. 33), or 1 chicken or vegetable stock cube dissolved in the same quantity of water

1 medium onion, peeled and chopped

1 clove garlic, peeled and crushed

½ teaspoon ground turmeric

1 teaspoon salt

½ teaspoon ground cinnamon

2 small green chillies, chopped

1 teaspoon grated maldive fish, salted fish or dried prawns (optional)

4 curry leaves (optional)

a 1 inch (2.5cm) piece *rampe* or pandanus (optional)

5oz (150g) block coconut cream

1 tablespoon lemon juice

1. Put the stock in a saucepan and add all the ingredients except for the coconut cream and lemon juice. Cook over a medium heat until the onions are tender.

2. Add the coconut cream and stir to dissolve. At the point of serving, add the lemon juice and stir again.

OPPOSITE *Clockwise from top:* Quick and Easy Naan Bread (page 82), Sambol Ulek (page 28), Lamb Kebabs in Coriander and Mint, with Lemon Yoghurt (page 104)

MULLIGATAWNY

THERE are as many recipes for Mulligatawny as there are for Cornish pasties. Some are elaborate and call for endless ingredients, while others are fairly simple. We hope the recipe below will become one of your favourites.

SERVES 4–6

1lb (450g) stewing beef, cut into approximately ½ inch (1cm) cubes
1lb (450g) soup bones (ask the butcher to chop these into small pieces)
2 medium onions, peeled and diced
2 tablespoons very finely sliced ginger
6 cloves garlic, peeled and crushed
16 black peppercorns
1 teaspoon ground cumin

2 teaspoons ground coriander
¼ teaspoon ground turmeric
2 teaspoons salt
1 medium onion, peeled and sliced
1 tablespoon vegetable oil
8oz (250g) potatoes, peeled and cut into very small dice
3oz (75g) block coconut cream
1 tablespoon lemon or lime juice

1. Put all the ingredients, except the sliced onion, oil, potatoes, coconut cream and lemon or lime juice, in a large saucepan. Add 3 pints (1.7 litres) water, bring to the boil and skim off any froth. Reduce the heat, cover and simmer for 2 hours (or 15 minutes in a pressure cooker).

2. Strain the stock, saving the diced onions and pieces of meat.

3. Fry the sliced onion in the oil, add the meat, diced onions and the potatoes, and stir-fry until just turning brown.

4. Return the stock to the saucepan or pressure cooker, add the onion mixture and bring to the boil. Simmer for about 10 minutes or until the potatoes are just cooked.

5. Add the coconut cream and lemon or lime juice just before serving. Take care not to boil the soup again or it may curdle.

VARIATION

✦ Like most Sri Lankan or Asian dishes, this one is improved by the addition of a 2 inch (5cm) piece of pandanus (*rampe*) leaf or 4 curry leaves to the stock. Although not essential, they impart a delicious flavour.

RASAM

PEPPER WATER

ORIGINATING from India, *Rasam* is a thin acidic soup, very peppery and hot, which is drunk during the main meal or poured over dry rice and curries. Many believe it stops the pain of indigestion – and hangovers! It is excellent for cutting through the richness of many curries.

SERVES 4

2oz (50g) dried tamarind
12 black peppercorns (or 2 teaspoons ground black pepper but ensure it is fresh)
½ medium onion, peeled
2 cloves garlic, peeled and crushed

1 teaspoon salt
1 teaspoon ground cumin
2 teaspoons vegetable oil
2 teaspoons whole mustard seeds, slightly crushed
3 curry leaves (optional)

1. Pour 1 pint (570ml) hot water over the tamarind and leave to soak. When cool, strain to remove the seeds and any pith.

2. Crush the peppercorns and chop the onion finely. Put all the ingredients, except the oil, mustard seeds and curry leaves, in a saucepan and bring to the boil. Turn the heat down and simmer for 15 minutes.

3. Put the oil in a frying pan and, when hot, add the mustard seeds (and curry leaves if using). When the seeds 'pop', remove the pan from the heat, add the contents of the other saucepan, and serve.

VARIATION

✦ If liked, add 2 tablespoons red lentils, and 1 tablespoon diced raw potatoes with the onions. Boil the *Rasam* until they are cooked, adding more water if necessary.

EGG DROP SOUP

YOU WILL come across different varieties of Egg Drop Soup in every Chinese restaurant across the globe. Once you know how easy it is to prepare, you can let your imagination run riot by adding all sorts of ingredients (see Variations, below). Unlike the clear soups usually served in Thailand and Indonesia, this one has a thickened base so it is more substantial.

When cooking for a dinner party, prepare the soup up to step 2 and set aside. Then you need only allow 3 minutes for step 3 onwards – what could be easier or quicker?

SERVES 4

1¾ pints (1 litre) Homemade Chicken Stock (p. 33) or 2 good chicken or vegetable stock cubes dissolved in the same quantity of water

1 slice (about 1 teaspoon) ginger, cut into very fine slivers

1 tablespoon cornflour, mixed to a cream with 2 tablespoons water

2 eggs, lightly beaten

3 spring onions, washed, trimmed and finely chopped

1 teaspoon sherry or ginger wine to taste

⅛ teaspoon ground white pepper

salt (optional)

1. Put the stock and ginger into a large saucepan and bring to the boil. Simmer for 10 minutes, then check the seasoning and adjust if necessary.

2. Slowly pour in the cornflour mixture, stirring well. Boil until the soup becomes clear and thickens.

3. Add the beaten eggs, stirring well, and take off the heat. The egg should begin to form strands in the soup.

4. Add the spring onions, sherry or ginger wine, and pepper, taste and add salt if needed.

5. Serve immediately. This soup cannot be reheated.

VARIATIONS

✦ Add 3 crab sticks, cut in half and shredded.

✦ Add 3oz (75g) each: shredded cooked chicken and cucumber pieces; or shredded ham and lettuce; or ½ can creamed sweetcorn and chopped cooked chicken breast; or any variation of diced ham, meat, fish or seafood.

TOM YUM KUNG

SPICY SHRIMP & LEMON SOUP

THIS clear Thai soup has its cousin in nearly every country that borders the Pacific. Its wonderful contrasting hot and sour flavours reflect the best of South-East Asian cuisine. If you can take it hotter, by all means add more chillies but do take care! We have given double the normal recipe because we know you will want to save some for the freezer.

SERVES 6–8

2lb (1kg) large shrimps or prawns in their shells
1 stalk of lemon grass, chopped, or
  1 teaspoon grated lime or lemon rind
¼ teaspoon grated galangal or ginger
2 fresh red chillies, chopped
1 tablespoon fish sauce

2–3 tablespoons lime or lemon juice (try the smaller amount first, adding more at step 5 if necessary)
3 spring onions, washed, trimmed and chopped
2 tablespoons chopped coriander leaves

1. Take the shells and heads off the shrimps or prawns. Save the meat.

2. Put the shells, heads, 3 pints (1.7 litres) water and all the ingredients, except the prawn meat, spring onions and coriander leaves, into a large saucepan and bring to the boil.

3. Simmer for 10 minutes, then strain the stock.

4. Wash out the saucepan, return the stock to it, bring to the boil and add the prawn meat.

5. Warm the soup through, then just before serving add the spring onions and coriander leaves. Taste and adjust the seasoning.

VARIATIONS

✦ If you can get hold of 2 kaffir lime leaves, add these to the stock at step 2. They really do bring out the citrus flavour.

✦ Add some *Sambol Ulek* (p. 28) if you want to zap your taste buds well and truly!

MIXED VEGETABLE & WONTON SOUP

THIS clear broth, served with either Wontons or meat balls, is one of our easiest and most delicious soup recipes. It is also the one most requested by our family and friends. Needless to say we don't mind preparing it because it is so easy and gives us more time to escape from the kitchen and chat to our loved ones.

This is a very substantial soup which can make a light lunch or supper dish on its own.

SERVES 4–5

20 stuffed Wontons (p. 46) or 2 large premium sausages taken out of their skins and 1 tablespoon cornflour

2 pints (1.2 litres) Homemade Chicken Stock (p. 33) or 2 good chicken stock cubes dissolved in the same quantity of water

2 teaspoons soy sauce

1 teaspoon sherry

2oz (50g) cucumber, cut into very fine matchsticks

4oz (110g) mixed sliced vegetables (this is an ideal way to use up any leftovers from previous recipes, e.g. use water chestnuts, mushrooms and bamboo shoots)

1oz (25g) vermicelli or cellophane noodles, cut with scissors into 2 inch (5cm) lengths and soaked in water

⅛ teaspoon ground white pepper

1. If using the Wontons, prepare them and set aside. If using the pork balls, form the sausagemeat into very small balls and roll them in the cornflour to prevent them sticking together. Set aside.

2. Put the stock, soy sauce and sherry in a large saucepan and bring to the boil.

3. Add the cucumber and mixed vegetables and boil for 1 minute.

4. Add the vermicelli and Wontons or pork balls and boil for another 2 minutes or until the Wontons or pork balls rise to the surface.

5. Stir in the pepper and serve immediately.

VARIATIONS

✦ Sprinkle with 1 chopped spring onion.

✦ If you can get it, ½ teaspoon *tung choi* (preserved Chinese vegetable) adds a real boost – stir it in at the end.

Melon with chicken & ham

Use Chinese winter melon if available, or young marrows, de-seeded cucumbers, or even the white flesh between the rind and red flesh of watermelon. When we were small, Mum would cut the red flesh off the melon, give it to us in bowls and save the prized white flesh. We weren't trusted with the normal slices on the rind because we would invariably forget, and eat the juicy flesh right down to the green skin. Besides using it in this soup, she would cut the white melon flesh into small dice and stir-fry it with strips of pork, onions and chillies in soy sauce – absolutely scrumptious!

This is a basic Vietnamese soup but similar dishes are found in Chinese, Japanese and other Oriental cuisines.

SERVES 6

1lb (450g) raw chicken (on the bone and cut into small serving pieces)

6 spring onions, washed, trimmed and chopped

½ teaspoon ground black pepper

3 pints (1.7 litres) Homemade Chicken Stock (p. 33) or water

2lb (1kg) winter melon (or see above for variations), peeled, sliced and cut into small chunks (use only the firm flesh – discard any spongy bits and the seeds)

1 tablespoon fish sauce

4oz (110g) ham, cut into quite small but thick matchsticks

1 teaspoon salt

1. Put the chicken, spring onions, pepper and stock or water into a large saucepan and bring to the boil.

2. Cover and simmer for 1 hour (or 15 minutes in a pressure cooker).

3. Add the melon, fish sauce, ham and salt, and boil for 1 minute only. Taste, adjust the seasoning, and serve.

VARIATIONS

✦ We confess to using our good old standby, 3 chicken stock cubes with 1 teaspoon *tung choi* (preserved Chinese vegetable) instead of making our own stock when pushed for time. It still tastes delicious!

✦ If you wish, you can substitute the same weight of pork belly or stewing beef for the chicken.

Rice

How we love rice! We confess that no meal is really complete for us without it. On returning from holiday, Rani has been known to head immediately for the kitchen and the rice boiler, no matter what gourmet food has been available. Rice deprivation is a serious thing.

Mother always made us eat every grain and we never ever threw it away. According to the Chinese, rice is the most labour-intensive crop and should be treated with great respect. It takes seven people to bring it to your table: one to plant the seed; one to tend the plants; one to harvest; one to mill; one to transport it; one to cook it; and one to serve it. Their efforts should not be taken lightly.

In the paddy fields, the workers are up to their knees in water, and water buffaloes are used to help with the heavy work. All sorts of little creatures can be found in the fields – small fishes, freshwater crustaceans and frogs, all of which provide a useful supplement to the diet of the poor.

There are a number of different rices in the East: white long-grain (Patna) and basmati are well known, and Thai fragrant rice is appearing on more dining tables. But what about trying unmilled red or country rice, or highly desirable small-grained samba, for a change? Most of these unusual rices absorb more water than ordinary Western rices – some of them up to double the quantity.

Cooking Rice

We prepare rice in the traditional manner – washing the grains under plenty of fresh running water until the water thrown away runs clear (this ensures the starch is rinsed out – along with the vitamins, alas, but this is how we do it back home).

To cook long-grain rice, put the rice in a saucepan, and add enough water to cover. Next, point your index finger directly at the rice, rest the finger at right angles to the surface and add enough water to reach the second joint of your finger. Bring the rice to the boil and boil fiercely until most of the water has evaporated (about 10–15 minutes) and little 'volcanoes' of escaping steam blow bubbles on the surface. Immediately cover with a tight-fitting lid, lower the heat and simmer for 10 minutes. Then turn the heat off and let the rice absorb any moisture by leaving it to rest for 10 minutes.

To cook small-grained rice, like samba, the water should come up to the knuckle.

The best way to ensure separate fluffy grains of rice every time is to invest in an electric rice boiler. You can pick them up for about £30 and, once you have one, you will really wonder how you ever managed without it. If you like trouble-free entertaining or just want a foolproof way to cook rice, there is no better piece of equipment to invest in. Every Oriental or Asian family owns one – and most of them have a simple keep-warm facility which is ideal for staggered meals when the family comes in at different times.

YELLOW RICE

❀

A LARGE platter of saffron–flavoured yellow rice is the centrepiece of any Sri Lankan party. Put the rice on a large oval platter and decorate with quartered hard-boiled eggs. Sprinkle over golden fried onions, salted cashew nuts, sultanas and peas and serve.

SERVES 4–6

4oz (110g) butter or ghee
a few strands of saffron soaked in a little warm milk *or* 2 teaspoons ground turmeric
4 cloves
a 2 inch (5cm) piece of cinnamon stick
5 green cardamom pods, bruised
1 stalk of lemon grass
1 teaspoon salt
15 black peppercorns
1lb (450g) samba or long-grain rice
3½ oz (100g) block coconut cream mixed to a thick cream with 4 tablespoons warm water

1 pint (570ml) Homemade Chicken Stock (p. 33) or 2 good chicken or vegetable stock cubes dissolved in the same quantity of hot water

Garnish
4 eggs, hard-boiled
1 large onion, peeled and cut into very thin rings
vegetable oil
2oz (50g) peas, either fresh or frozen
4oz (110g) each salted cashew nuts and sultanas

1. Melt the butter or ghee in a large saucepan over a low heat. Add the dry ingredients and rice, and stir until each grain of rice is coated.

2. Add the coconut cream, stock, and saffron in milk if using. Bring to the boil, then turn down the heat and simmer. Stir occasionally until the rice is cooked.

3. Meanwhile, prepare the garnish. Shell the hard-boiled eggs and cut each one into 4 (or 8 if large) segments. Fry the onion rings in a little oil until golden brown and set aside. Put the peas in a saucepan, cover them with water and bring to the boil for only a few seconds. Then plunge them into ice cold water and drain to keep them green and *al dente* ('with a bite', as the Italians say about spaghetti).

4. Remove as many whole spices from the rice as possible, turn out onto a large platter and garnish with the hard-boiled eggs, onion rings, peas, cashew nuts and sultanas.

MILK RICE

A T Sinhala (Sri Lankan) New Year, our cook would make *kiri bath* or milk rice. Part of the ritual would be to boil a small quantity of milk on the stove until it overflowed. This would guarantee good health and good fortune for the family. We always remember waking each Sinhala New Year's Day to the smell of burning milk accompanied by the loud bang of firecrackers. *Kiri bath* is also served for breakfast on the first day of each lunar month.

This recipe requires country rice which is a lovely red colour. It needs more liquid and a slightly longer cooking time than white long-grain rice.

SERVES 4–6

1lb (450g) white or unmilled country rice	3½oz (100g) block coconut cream
3 teaspoons salt	butter to grease dish

1. Wash the rice, place in a saucepan with 1 pint (570ml) water and the salt and bring to the boil.

2. Boil for about 10–15 minutes, then add the coconut cream mixed to a cream with 1fl oz (30ml) hot water.

3. Cover the pan with a tight-fitting lid, lower the heat and simmer for 10–15 minutes.

4. Turn off the heat but leave covered for another 5 minutes.

5. Butter a shallow flat dish, turn the rice into it and smooth the surface. Use a potato masher to mark the top of the rice in a pattern if liked.

6. Mark the rice into diamonds or squares with 2 inch (5cm) sides and serve in the dish, with *Seeni Sambol* (p. 37), Coconut Sambol (p. 34) and Salt Fish Curry (p. 121).

CHICKEN RICE

SIDLE UP to a Malaysian or Singaporean and whisper 'Chicken Rice' in their ear. They will adopt a yearning expression, their eyes will glaze over with remembered pleasure, and homesickness will definitely strike. If you visit this part of the world ask any taxi driver where you can get this dish. Everyone has their own favourite haunt.

Eating out here includes visiting the many hawker stands dotted by the roadside. People with gas cylinders and woks or metal trays will serve the freshest, most delicious food imaginable. There are food centres where you sit in the middle on tables and chairs. Around the sides will be stalls selling Chinese, Indian and Malaysian or Thai specialities, cakes, desserts and freshly made fruit juices. The cooks will come over to you, you choose what you want to eat and drink from the vast selection available, then pay at the end. We always order this dish.

Any leftover stock makes an ideal base for many of the soup and noodle recipes in this book. The meat from the chicken carcass is ideal for many of the stir-fry recipes too.

SERVES 4

1 × 3lb 4oz (1.5kg) chicken (preferably free-range – corn-fed is very good)	2 teaspoons *tung choi* (preserved Chinese vegetable, optional)
2 chicken stock cubes	4 slices fresh ginger
3 black peppercorns, crushed	8oz (225g) long-grain rice
½ lemon, cut into slices	1 cucumber, cut into batons (see opposite)

1. Put the chicken, breast-side down, in a deep pot with a lid; a pressure cooker is ideal.

2. Dissolve the stock cubes in 4½ pints (2.5 litres) boiling water. Pour the stock over the chicken (it should just cover the bird), add all the ingredients except the rice and cucumber, and bring to the boil and cover. If you have the giblets, add them to the water to intensify the flavour. Boil for 10 minutes, turn the heat down, simmer for another 20 minutes, then turn the heat off. *Do not lift the lid off* but leave the chicken to cool for at least 4 hours. By that time it should be perfectly cooked, and not dry in the slightest.

3. Drain the chicken and cut the succulent meat into serving portions. Keep warm.

4. Fish out the ginger and lemon slices and discard. Save the stock.

5. Rinse the rice several times until the water runs clear. Leaving this stage out will mean healthier but less appetising rice.

6. Put the rice in a pan with a tight-fitting lid. Add enough chicken stock to cover the rice, then enough extra stock to come 1 inch (2.5cm) up the side of the pan. Bring the rice to the boil, then cover and simmer until perfectly cooked. Resist the urge to peek, so that the steam is retained in the pan.

7. Serve the chicken on a bed of rice with cucumber batons and some bottled chilli sauce.

8. To make cucumber batons, wash the cucumber, hold it vertically and drag a fork down the sides, turning frequently to make ridges or stripes down the whole fruit. Cut the cucumber into 2 inch (5cm) pieces, then into thick matchsticks.

VARIATION

✦ If you are lucky enough to track down Szechuan peppercorns, crush 1 tablespoon sea salt and 1 tablespoon peppercorns together and serve in a small bowl. Guests take a pinch and sprinkle on their serving of Chicken Rice.

Biriyani

SAVOURY RICE WITH MEAT

Our father's mother would spin in her grave if she knew he had become an ace cook. Theirs was a typical Edwardian home, with strict demarcation lines between servants and family. The family (of four) had a gardener, driver, maid and cook and it would have been quite unusual for a member of the family to do any manual work.

Grandfather, Francis Cooray, was a journalist, like our father, Dodwell. Francis was very respected in his field – Sports Editor for the *Malay Mail*, and South-East Asian Correspondent for many years for Reuters and the *Financial Times*, London. Dad has inherited much of his generosity of spirit and is one of life's true gentlemen, as well as being very modest. Now his greatest pleasure is having the family round for meals and this is one of the special dishes that we always ask him to prepare for us.

Leftover Biriyani freezes well but leave out the eggs.

SERVES 6–8

1lb (450g) boned lamb or beef, chopped into 1 inch (2.5cm) cubes
1 tablespoon malt vinegar
2 teaspoons ground coriander
3 teaspoons ground cumin
1 teaspoon ground turmeric
2 teaspoons salt
1 teaspoon ground black pepper
2lb (1kg) Patna or samba rice
8oz (250g) ghee (concentrated or cooking butter from the supermarket is quite acceptable)

4oz (110g) onions, peeled and sliced
3 cloves garlic, peeled and crushed
a 2 inch (5cm) piece of ginger, peeled and crushed
6 cardamom pods, lightly crushed
4 cloves
4oz (110g) ripe tomatoes, chopped
8 green chillies, chopped
6–8 hard-boiled eggs, shelled

1. Mix the meat with the vinegar, ground spices, salt and pepper and set aside.

2. Wash the rice in running water and set aside.

3. Heat the ghee in a pan, fry the onions, garlic and ginger until golden brown, then add the cardamom pods, cloves and meat. Keep stirring until all the liquid has evaporated and the meat begins to fry.

4. Add the rice, tomatoes, chillies and 1¾ pints (2 litres) water, bring to the boil and cook for 10–15 minutes. Put on a tight-fitting lid, reduce the heat and simmer until the rice is tender and the water has evaporated.

5. To serve, stir carefully so that the meat and vegetables are evenly distributed, turn out onto a platter and place the hard-boiled eggs in the rice so that each person has a generous helping of rice, meat and a whole egg.

VARIATION

♦ If liked, add Dry Potato and Coconut Curry (p. 140) to the rice. Served with a few vegetable curries and sambols, this makes a substantial meal in itself and is ideal for entertaining.

COMPRESSED RICE CAKES

THESE easy-to-prepare individual portions of rice are served with Thai, Malaysian and Japanese dishes. They can be flavoured by adding a number of different ingredients.

Make them the day before and store in the refrigerator. They can also be frozen on trays and defrosted a few at a time when needed. It's useful to keep an emergency supply for entertaining or when you fancy something different.

Use the same-sized cup to measure the rice and stock.

SERVES 4–6

2 cups pudding rice
4 cups chicken or vegetable stock (made
  with 2 stock cubes)

1 tablespoon grated fresh ginger *or* 5 kaffir
  lime leaves *or* the grated rind and juice
  of 2 lemons

1. Do not wash the rice but place all the ingredients in a pan with a tight-fitting lid. Bring to the boil, lower the heat and cook for about 30 minutes or until the rice is cooked and all the liquid has been absorbed.

2. Turn the rice into a well-oiled metal tray measuring about 6 × 10 inches (16 × 26cm), cover with 2 sheets of foil and press down with a number of heavy weights – hardback books, cans, even full wine bottles! You want to compress the rice, so use quite heavy objects.

3. Leave overnight in the fridge.

4. Using a sharp knife, cut the rice into squares or diamond shapes. If the rice sticks, wet the blade in water. Turn out carefully and serve with curries or Simple Malay Beef Satay (p. 95).

Chok

CHINESE WATERY RICE

PLEASE DO not shudder and quickly turn the page. Most Chinese eat *Chok* for breakfast and, as there are several million of them, we reckon more people in the world sit down to this dish than cereal or porridge or even Britain's beloved bacon and eggs. Although it may be a bit much asking you to start the day off with this dish, it is quite delicious served as a light supper dish or when someone is off their food. It is good for convalescents as it is easily digested. Teamed up with Golden Coin Eggs (p. 118), it was one of Rani's favourite childhood meals.

Mum would often decant the remnants of our fridge into *chok* and then it became *bobo* – a very hit-and-miss family special. If we had curry, this went in, as well as any bits of stir-fries. It could be absolutely delicious and then again . . . We well remember a day when she was in more of a hurry than usual. *That* particular *bobo* had two ham sandwiches floating in it – not to be recommended! Finely shredded cooked meat, chicken or fish are fine.

SERVES 2–3

8oz (250g) cooked rice

2 pints (1.2 litres) water or Homemade Chicken Stock (p. 33) or 2 good chicken or vegetable stock cubes dissolved in the same quantity of water

1 teaspoon salt

2 teaspoons *tung choi* (preserved Chinese vegetable)

a little ground white pepper (optional)

soy sauce (optional)

a few spring onions, washed, trimmed and finely chopped

1. Put the rice in a saucepan with all the ingredients except the pepper, soy sauce and spring onions.

2. Bring to the boil, reduce the heat, cover and simmer for about 30 minutes. The rice should have turned into something resembling very thin porridge.

3. Taste and adjust the seasoning. Add a little white ground pepper, extra salt or soy sauce if liked, sprinkle the chopped spring onions on top, and serve.

Breads & Pancakes

Although we confess to loving rice more than anything else, we are rather fond of the recipes we share with you in this chapter. The flours we use are ordinary plain or self-raising (white) wheat flour, ground rice or rice flour. All are freely available in supermarkets or local shops. Like wholewheat flour, unmilled rice flour has a characteristic reddish colour.

Back home the raising agent for *Thosais* (p. 81) and Hoppers (p. 74) would be toddy (fermented coconut water) which gives a slightly sour taste. However, through trial and error, we discovered that we got almost the same result in a much shorter time by using easy-mix instant yeast. If you are really impatient do as we do and warm the flour before adding the yeast and liquid. A couple of minutes on low power in the microwave (taking care not to scorch or kill it) really gets that yeast going.

We also use yeast in our *Pao* (Chinese dumpling) recipe (p. 78), although you will doubtless come across cooks who advocate using plain flour and boiling water. Ours come out fluffy and light and Mum, Dad and the kids prefer them to the more traditional variety which are rather heavy.

Everything in this chapter can be frozen if wrapped well, except for Hoppers. The craze for miniaturising food (baby vegetables especially) is still going strong. We have been amused to see tiny individual portions of fish and chips wrapped in small sheets of newspaper, and tiny doner kebabs or bite-sized hamburgers appearing at some smart parties. We have often done the same with our Naan Bread (p. 82) and *Paos* (p. 78).

Incidentally for those travellers tempted by our stories to track down some genuine Sri Lankan toddy (our native hooch), please make sure you examine its origins very carefully. Without wishing to malign toddy-makers in general, we have seen all sorts of unsavoury unwanted protein (dead insects and worse) floating in the buckets of less reputable manufacturers ...

SRI LANKAN HOPPERS

A HOPPER (or *appa*) is a crisp concave 'pancake' with a spongy centre. In Sri Lanka these bowl-shaped savouries used to appear from breakfast until the early hours of the morning. Eaten with Coconut Sambol (p. 34), curries and lentils, or even jam or honey, they are one of the finest dishes we know. Many people have a balti pan (like a small wok) lurking in the back of the cupboard. They are perfect for making Hoppers, so drag them out, dust them off and have a go. If you do not possess a balti pan you can use the same mixture to make pancakes in a small frying pan. They will not look the same, although they will taste just as good.

Hoppers (and their lacy rice-flour cousins, Stringhoppers or strings, p. 88) are the staple breakfast dish for most Sri Lankans. They were the speciality of the fisher folk who lived on the beach near our house, and we would order them the night before. They would arrive early in the morning, in a flat basket, covered with clean banana leaves still warm from the fire, with a small newspaper cone nestling underneath containing fiery Coconut Sambol. Delicious and costing just a few cents, they were the things we mourned most when we came to the West. Just like we pined for Marmite, Walls bacon and sausages, and baked beans when we returned home!

Hoppers are best eaten fresh – tipped out of the pan onto someone's waiting plate – although you can keep them in an airtight container for the next day.

There is a definite skill to making these – judging how much oil to use to grease the pan, the consistency of the mixture and how long to cook it. Like all pancakes, once you master the knack you will never forget it. If your first attempt fails, just throw it out, wipe the pan with oiled paper or cloth and try again.

MAKES 20–24; *enough for 6–8*

12oz (350g) ground rice (white or the unmilled 'red' variety)	1 × ¼oz (6g) packet easy-blend instant dried yeast
12oz (350g) rice flour or plain white flour	1½ teaspoons sugar
1 × 7oz (200g) block coconut cream, cut into small cubes	2 teaspoons salt
	1 teaspoon malt vinegar
	oil, to grease frying pan

1. Mix all the ingredients except the oil in a deep bowl, together with 2½ pints (1.5 litres) hand-hot water, and leave in a warm place until thick and frothy and doubled in size. Sri Lankans start it off the night before, if Hoppers are on the menu for breakfast. The batter should be like pouring cream, but thin enough to form a transparent 'skin' up the sides of the pan. Only trial and error will give you the right consistency, and every batch will be different according to the flour used (or even the weather!).

2. Brush a balti pan or deep frying pan with oil and heat on a gas or electric ring. When the oil smokes, pour in a tablespoonful of batter. Using a thick cloth, pick up the pan with both hands and roll it until the sides are coated about two-thirds of the way up.

3. Cover with a tight-fitting lid or ovenproof plate and cook over a very low heat for 5 minutes or until the sides are brown and the centre is set.

4. Use a metal spatula to gently ease the hopper from the sides of the pan and slip it out onto a plate. Oil the pan and continue until all the mixture is used up.

5. Hoppers should be crisp on the outside and soft and spongy in the middle.

VARIATION

✦ To make an **egg hopper**, break an egg into the uncooked hopper at the end of stage 2 of the above recipe. Cover and cook over a low heat, as described above, until the egg is set.

COCONUT ROTIS

THIS ROUND flat bread or pancake flavoured with coconut is very simple to make but deliciously different. When we were not gorging on Hoppers or 'strings' it made a good breakfast alternative. After lessons had ended at the Methodist College for Girls, Colombo, in the early afternoon, we would go over to Aunty Lulu's in Colpetty and wait for Dad to pick us up after work. Aunty Lulu's cook and *amah* made the most delicious afternoon tiffin or snacks. Although we were both very chubby, we would try very hard to suck in our cheeks and look like starving waifs. This trick usually worked and nearly every day we were invited by our soft-hearted cousins Sonia and Aloma to join them for tea. Their *amah* made the best *rotis* in the world.

Rotis will freeze but are best eaten hot and fresh.

MAKES 16; *enough for 6–8*

1lb (450g) self-raising wheat flour or rice flour (use 1 teaspoon baking powder sifted with the rice flour)
4oz (110g) desiccated coconut (fine cut)
1 teaspoon salt

1 small green chilli, chopped
4 curry leaves, crumbled (optional)
1 egg, whisked
1 tablespoon oil, to grease frying pan

1. Mix all the dry ingredients in a bowl, add the egg, then add 7–9fl oz (200–250ml) water, a little at a time, to form a stiff dough.

2. Knead for a few moments on a floured surface, then put the dough into an oiled bag (see *Pao* recipe, step 3, p. 78) and leave in a warm place for about 45 minutes.

3. Divide the dough into 16 equal balls, then roll each into a circle about the size of a saucer, on a floured surface.

4. Lightly grease a heavy frying pan and cook over a medium heat for about 4 minutes. Turn over and cook on the other side.

VARIATION

✦ If liked, add ½ teaspoon grated maldive fish to the mixture before adding the water.

ROTI DJALA

LACY INDONESIAN PANCAKES

THESE DELICATE filigree circles echo the ornate moulding found in Oriental temples. They are traditionally made by dipping the fingers of one hand in the batter, then letting it fall in four steady strings. But a satisfactory effect can be gained by using a small teaspoon and pouring a steady thin stream of batter in random patterns across a hot frying pan.

In Sri Lanka we would use a small tuft of coconut husk (*copra*) dipped in oil to grease a pan or hopper mould. Now we make do with a piece of paper towel or a clean rag.

These pancakes are served with dry curries and sambols.

SERVES 4–6

2oz (50g) block coconut cream
8oz (225g) plain flour
2 eggs, beaten

½ teaspoon salt
oil, to grease frying pan

1. Dissolve the coconut cream in 13fl oz (375ml) hot water.

2. Use a blender or whisk to mix all the ingredients, except the oil, into a smooth lump-free batter.

3. Heat a lightly greased frying pan. When it starts to smoke dip your fingers (or a teaspoon) into the batter and move across the pan to resemble a lace pattern. Do not make it too full of holes or you will have difficulty scooping up your curry with the completed pancake!

4. Turn the pancake over and cook for a couple of seconds until it begins to brown at the edges. Repeat until all the batter is used up. The batter may be thicker as you come to the bottom of the bowl. If so, just add a little water to thin it down.

P_{AO}

STUFFED STEAMED CHINESE DUMPLINGS

THERE ARE four main regions in China, the cuisine of each reflecting its climate and harvest. Beijing (Peking) cuisine dominates the northern region. This area specialises in locally grown wheat products such as pancakes, buns (*pao*), and *zchotse*, a soft deep-fried bread stick like a salty doughnut. Meats are served with rich sweet and sour sauces and dips based on red beans. The best known dish from this area is, of course, Peking Duck.

Pao are steamed stuffed bread dumplings which can be made in different sizes. We favour smaller ones, about 1½ inches (4cm) in diameter. Two of these, served with a selection of chilli and sweet and sour sauces, make a delicious starter. Make a double quantity and freeze in individual plastic bags. When you fancy a late-night TV snack just defrost and enjoy them with a choice of sauces and chilli dips.

MAKES 12; *enough for 6*

DUMPLINGS

3fl oz (75ml) milk	1 teaspoon sugar
8oz (225g) self-raising flour	¼ teaspoon salt
⅛ oz (3g) or ½ packet instant easy-blend dried yeast	oil

1. Mix the milk with 3fl oz (75ml) boiling water in a large bowl. Add the rest of the ingredients and mix to a soft dough.

2. Turn out onto a floured surface. Knead until the ball of dough becomes smooth and elastic.

3. Put the dough in a large oiled plastic bag. To oil the bag, place 1 teaspoon oil inside it and rub together until all the inside surfaces are covered. Tie a knot at the top giving the dough plenty of room to rise. Leave to double in size in a warm place. You will find this method is quick and simple – try it for proving traditional yeast-based Western dough recipes, too.

4. Prepare the filling (see opposite, and page 80) and put aside to cool.

5. When the dough is spongy and light, open the bag and tip onto a floured surface. Divide into 12 balls.

6. Pat each ball out to a circle about the size of your palm. Put 1½ teaspoons filling in the middle, then gather the edges together and pinch to seal.

7. Turn the balls over, taking care not to let any of the filling escape.

8. Cut a circle of greaseproof paper the size of your steamer and line the top half. Place the dumplings on the paper-lined half, leaving plenty of space between them as they will double in size.

9. Steam over rapidly boiling water for 10–15 minutes until the dumplings are light, fluffy and cooked.

STIR-FRIED FILLING

8oz (225g) any leftover stir-fried vegetable or meat mixture

1 teaspoon cornflour (optional)
½ teaspoon sherry (optional)

1. If very watery, thicken the stir-fried filling with the cornflour mixed with the sherry and 1 tablespoon water.

2. Add to the filling and boil until thickened.

PORK FILLING

1 teaspoon oil
4oz (110g) sliced Char Sui Pork (p. 98)
2oz (50g) bamboo shoots

2oz (50g) bean sprouts
1 teaspoon cornflour
½ teaspoon sherry
1 teaspoon soy sauce

1. Heat the oil in a frying pan. Add the pork, bamboo shoots and bean sprouts and stir-fry for 2 minutes.

2. Mix the cornflour with the sherry, soy sauce and 1 tablespoon water.

3. Add to the filling and boil until thickened.

CHICKEN FILLING

1 tablespoon sliced onions

4oz (110g) sliced chicken breast (cooked or raw)

½ teaspoon oil

½ teaspoon sugar

1 teaspoon cornflour

½ teaspoon sherry

1 tablespoon soy sauce

⅛–½ teaspoon grated fresh ginger

1. Fry the onions and chicken in the oil.

2. Mix the sugar and cornflour with the sherry, soy sauce and 1 tablespoon water. Add to the filling, with the ginger, and boil until thickened.

THOSAIS

MALAYSIAN SAVOURY PANCAKES

ONE OF our kids' favourite uncles is Desmond, the retired general manager of Kuala Lumpur airport. They love him because he is always full of tricks and jokes (usually naughty ones). His wife, saintly Aunty Daisy, can only remonstrate with a gentle 'Must you, Desmond?' and he generally does!

When we stayed with Uncle Desmond he insisted on trying to get us to eat every Malaysian speciality known to man. Ignoring our weak protests, he would push us out of bed at 5.30am and drag us off to eat freshly made *thosais*.

Thosais are very popular in South India and Sri Lanka as well as Malaysia. As with all flour-based recipes it is difficult to give the exact amount of water needed for these savoury pancakes. Add more plain flour to the mixture if the batter seems too thin, or a little water if it is too thick. It should be like thick cream.

MAKES 24; *enough for 6*

4oz (110g) *urid dhal* (ask for these small black lentils at your local Asian or healthfood shop)
½ quantity Hopper mixture (p. 74)
2 teaspoons oil
½ teaspoon mustard seeds

2 curry leaves, crumbled (optional)
½ small onion, peeled and very finely chopped
2–3 teaspoons salt to taste
1 small green chilli, finely chopped
oil, to grease the frying pan

1. Soak the lentils overnight in at least 4 pints (2 litres) water. Next day, rinse well in fresh running water, then grind in a blender with 5fl oz (150ml) water. Add some of the hopper mixture if needed. The mixture should be a smooth lump-free paste.

2. Stir in the remaining hopper mixture and set aside.

3. Heat the oil in a frying pan, add the mustard seeds and curry leaves if used, and fry until the seeds pop. Add the chopped onion and fry until golden.

4. Mix the batter with the cooled onion mixture, salt and chilli, and stir well. Brush the base of a heavy frying pan with a little oil and spread 2 tablespoons batter over the pan with a metal spatula or the blade of a knife. Turn once, then cook on the other side.

5. Repeat until all the batter is used up, oiling the pan between each *thosai*. Eat freshly made with a selection of curries.

QUICK AND EASY NAAN BREAD

LIGHT FLUFFY *naans*, ready to be enhanced with your own toppings ... Although supermarkets stock this gorgeous bread, this recipe really is easy, so do try it.

Rani now lives in Walthamstow, close to an amazing tandoori takeaway. Run by an elderly husband and wife from their converted front room, it is unbelievably cheap. Customers are treated to a real double act as they argue over orders. Everything is freshly cooked and they bring out teaspoons for customers to taste and adjust the seasonings while their food is prepared. Fast food it is not!

Although their kitchen is small, it is immaculately clean and a huge electric tandoor oven takes pride of place. Made from a special stone, the inside resembles an Ali Baba basket. The wife rolls out the dough for the *naan*, then leans in and slaps the bread directly onto the heated walls of the tandoor. It hangs there, defying gravity, and after about 2 minutes she turns it with a long fork and bakes the other side. Almost instantly it puffs up in the scorching heat, and brown spots cover the surface.

The following method tries to simulate the tandoor. Make sure your oven is red hot before you put the trays in. You will need a separate oven and grill.

MAKES 6

1lb (450g) self-raising flour and ½ teaspoon baking powder, sifted together	4 tablespoons plain yoghurt
	2 eggs (size 3)
	3 tablespoons melted butter, to glaze
½ teaspoon salt	2 tablespoons black poppy or sesame seeds
2 tablespoons oil	(optional)

1. Mix all the ingredients, except the melted butter and poppy or sesame seeds, in a large bowl.

2. Add 4–5fl oz (110–150ml) water, a little at a time, kneading well between additions, to form a soft dough.

3. Put into an oiled bag (see *Pao* recipe, step 3, p. 78) and leave to rest for 30 minutes.

4. Preheat the oven to its highest temperature and place 2 heavy metal baking trays upside down in the oven to heat up. At the same time put the grill on its highest setting.

5. Divide the dough into 6 equal balls. Roll out on a floured surface into either a round or the more traditional tear shape.

6. Carefully take out the hot trays with oven gloves, slap 1–2 *naans* (depending on the size of your *naan* and tray) onto them and bake for about 3 minutes.

7. Remove from the oven and flash grill for 30 seconds to 1 minute.

8. Brush the top with melted butter, and if liked sprinkle with either poppy or sesame seeds.

9. Remove the *naan* from the tray, put it back in the oven to reheat, remove the other tray and repeat the process. With a little practice, you can get a production line of trays going in and out of the oven. The trays will be very hot so watch out for accidents when drafting in any helpers.

VARIATIONS

✦ Thinly slice 2 onions and fry in 2 teaspoons oil until just softened. At step 6, press the fried onions onto the top of the *naan* before taking, to make a sort of Asian pizza.

✦ Microwave or boil a medium-sized potato until half-cooked. Dice, and sauté in 1 teaspoon oil until just turning brown. Press into the *naan* dough at step 6, then sprinkle with a little sea salt, chilli powder and 1 teaspoon finely chopped coriander leaves before baking.

PEKING PANCAKES OR SPRING ROLL WRAPPERS

COMING from the fierce north of China, Mother grew up on *pao* and other wheat products, as well as the pancakes which accompany Peking duck. She tells of meals where small bamboo steamers with these pancakes in them would be brought to the table and guests and family would help themselves to a variety of fillings, roll the pancakes up and eat them with a dipping sauce.

The pancakes can be made the day before. Cover with clingfilm or foil so they do not dry out, and steam when ready to serve. If you want to serve these as Mother describes, we suggest you team them up with roast duck, Char Sui Pork (p. 98), cucumber batons (p. 69), shredded spring onion, lightly steamed Chinese cabbage, bean sprouts and mushrooms. Good sauces would be hoi sin or Quick Plum Sauce (p. 31), *Sambol Ulek* (p. 28) and Satay Sauce (p. 32). Or eat them with Vietnamese Fish Sauce (p. 29).

By sheer necessity (big party to cater for and not enough wrappers) we discovered that these pancakes make good spring roll wrappers, too.

MAKES 36; *enough for 6–8 as a main meal*
(or, if rolled out smaller, makes 50 mini-wrappers for a buffet)

1lb (450g) plain flour
½ teaspoon salt

1 teaspoon sesame seed oil
extra flour, to roll out pancakes

1. Sift the flour and salt into a large bowl

2. Combine 8–9fl oz (225–250ml) boiling water with the sesame seed oil, pour into the flour and mix to a soft dough.

3. Knead for 5–10 minutes on a floured surface until the dough becomes smooth. Cover and leave for 30 minutes.

4. Divide the dough into 36 or 50 equal-sized balls. Then roll each out on a floured surface until it is very thin (you should be able to see through them).

5. Heat a non-stick frying pan, then dry-fry the pancakes for a few seconds on either side. They will develop small brown spots when they are done.

6. Put in a steamer and steam for 10 minutes before serving.

Noodles

OODLES AND OODLES of wonderful noodles! Noodles come in all shapes and sizes, from the ubiquitous yellow egg noodles to the more unfamiliar white rice noodles. The Chinese claim that the Italians learned how to eat pasta from Marco Polo – once they had introduced him to this most popular food!

Some noodles are very thick (the better to soak up rich sauces) and others almost hair-thin. Rice sticks (*meehoon*) are a staple found all across South-East Asia. They are eaten in soup, deep-fried until crispy and served with a sauce, or stir-fried with almost every imaginable combination of ingredients.

A very unusual noodle is the cellophane, thread or bean vermicelli, made from mung beans. So fine and light you have trouble weighing it for recipes, it becomes slippery and transparent when boiled in hot soups or sauces. It is nourishing and easily digested and Thais often use it as an ingredient in their spring roll fillings. We advise you to cut it into manageable lengths before cooking, as it is impossible to do so when cooked.

When we were small we were embarrassed by the way our Chinese and Malaysian friends ate noodles and rice. A small bowl would be held close to the mouth and the noodles sucked up very noisily with a loud slurp. Rice would be shovelled in with a pair of chopsticks held close together. This was when our different backgrounds began to grate against each other. Though a mortal offence in Western society, eating this way is seen as good form in the Orient – in the same way as a loud belch at the end of a meal and a dirty tablecloth are considered compliments to the cook.

As we began to travel more extensively we became older, wiser and more tolerant, and can now slurp with the best of them!

LO MEIN

LONG-LIFE NOODLES WITH BEEF & VEGETABLES

WE NEVER met our Chinese grandfather – we only ever saw a photograph of a patrician-looking man in a silk gown with very high cheekbones and a fierce stare. This was our *Kung Kung* (grandfather). A Manchurian by birth, he brought his family to live within the gates of the Forbidden City in Peking. The family's diet was based on flour products and not rice. We well remember Chinese New Year and indeed 1 January. Mum would prepare a large dish of long-life noodles, partly to remember *Kung Kung* by but also to ensure that we all lived long and healthy lives. Well, Mum is still going strong at 87 so it must work!

SERVES 4–6

a pinch of salt

8oz (225g) dried egg noodles

1lb (450g) beef steak, cut into very thin strips

3 tablespoons soy sauce

2 teaspoons cornflour

2 tablespoons oil

4 spring onions, washed, trimmed and chopped, or 2 onions, peeled and thinly sliced

4oz (110g) bamboo shoots, sliced into strips

1 green chilli, chopped (optional)

2 teaspoons sugar

1 tablespoon hoi sin sauce

4oz (110g) bean sprouts

1. Put 4 pints (2 litres) water in a large saucepan over a high heat. Add a pinch of salt and, when boiling, drop in the egg noodles. Cook for 8–10 minutes or according to the directions on the packet. Drain and set aside.

2. Toss the meat in 1 tablespoon soy sauce mixed with the cornflour. Keep to one side.

3. Heat the oil in a wok and, when smoking, stir-fry the spring onions and then the beef. Cook, stirring continuously, until the beef changes colour.

4. Add the bamboo shoots, chilli if using, sugar, hoi sin sauce, the rest of the soy sauce, and the bean sprouts. Stir-fry for 1 minute.

5. Lastly, add the noodles and toss so that all the ingredients are well mixed.

VARIATION
✦ This makes a very good vegetarian dish. Omit the beef and substitute 4oz (110g) each of carrot sticks, shredded *pak choi* (Chinese cabbage), mushrooms and ½ teaspoon *Sambol Ulek* (p. 28).

*E*ASIEST MIXED FRIED NOODLES EVER

*I*F YOU live within walking distance of a supermarket with a deli counter you could be eating this in 5 minutes – really!

SERVES 4–6

8oz (225g) three-minute egg noodles or
   ordinary spaghetti
salt
4oz (110g) each cooked ham, sliced
   chicken breast and roast beef
1 tablespoon oil
1 clove garlic, peeled and crushed

1 large onion, peeled and finely sliced
2oz (50g) water chestnuts, cut into
   quarters
4oz (110g) bean sprouts
2 teaspoons Thai Red Curry Paste 1 or 2
   (pp. 22–23)

1. Boil the noodles or spaghetti according to the directions on the packet in plenty of salted boiling water. Drain and keep warm.

2. Meanwhile cut the sliced meats into thin strips and set aside.

3. Put the oil into a pre-heated wok, heat and add the garlic and onion. Stir-fry for 2 minutes.

4. Add the water chestnuts, bean sprouts and meat and warm through for a few moments. Add the noodles and curry paste. Check the seasoning, adding a pinch of salt if necessary.

5. Serve on a large tray and tuck in!

VARIATION
✦ The discerning cook will seize on this recipe as a way of using up leftover joints of meat and quite rightly so! To give it a new twist, add a splash of ginger wine or sherry.

Mock stringhoppers

SOME OF our best times in Sri Lanka were the regular weekend dances at the Otters' Swimming Club (where we would bump into life member Arthur C. Clarke) or at the Dutch Burgher Union. A live band, complete with groovy saxophone, meeting our schoolfriends and relations of all ages, dancing under the stars, the air full of flickering fireflies and chirping crickets – and then the drive home, stopping on the way at some roadside *kade* (eating shack) where someone would be steaming crisp stringhoppers over an open fire and serving them with searingly hot curries.

Unless you have a village *kade*, or someone prepared to spend about three hours in the kitchen roasting rice flour, sifting it, making the paste, squeezing it out through a mould in strings onto individual mats and steaming it (oh really!), it's much better to try our mock stringhoppers.

'Strings' are a much-loved dish in Sri Lanka, and can be eaten for breakfast, lunch or dinner.

SERVES 6

1 × 1lb (450g) packet Chinese rice sticks   salt
(*meehoon*)

1. Bring a very large pan of salted water to the boil, drop in the rice sticks and stir to separate.

2. Boil for only 2 minutes, then immediately strain off the water. Put the rice sticks in an ovenproof dish and place in a steamer.

3. Steam for 5 minutes and serve with *Hodi* (p. 57), omelette, Coconut Sambol (p. 34), *Seeni Sambol* (p. 37), *Mallung* (p. 138) and any curries you wish.

TRANSPARENT NOODLES WITH MUSHROOMS & PORK OR PRAWNS

PEA STARCH noodles are also called transparent noodles. They are very easy to digest and slippery to eat. Because they are so light it is difficult to weigh them. Try making a ring out of your thumb and index finger and gather a bunch of noodles about that diameter for this recipe. Use a pair of scissors to cut the dry noodles into manageable pieces.

SERVES 3–4

2oz (50g) transparent noodles

4 tablespoons oil

4 spring onions, washed, trimmed and chopped

8oz (225g) minced pork, or 8oz (225g) fresh good-quality prawns, shelled and roughly chopped

4oz (110g) button mushrooms, wiped and sliced

½ teaspoon *Sambol Ulek* (p. 28) or Tabasco sauce

2 tablespoons soy sauce

1 tablespoon sherry

grated rind of 1 lemon

salt

a pinch of five spice powder

1. Soak the noodles in plenty of lukewarm water for 30 minutes, drain and set aside.

2. Heat the oil in a wok, then stir-fry the spring onions, pork or prawns, and mushrooms for 3 minutes.

3. Add the noodles and the rest of the ingredients, except the salt and five spice powder, and boil until the liquid has evaporated.

4. Pile onto a warmed dish, season to taste with salt, sprinkle with the five spice powder and serve with rice.

FRIED RICE STICKS WITH SEAFOOD & VEGETABLES

THE EASIEST meals can be prepared by using economical *meehoon* or rice sticks. These noodles need no cooking – just soak for about 30 minutes in warm water, drain and they are ready to be stir-fried with any of the meat or vegetable recipes in this book.

Meehoon is an ideal standby when catering for unexpected visitors. Bundles of the white string-like noodles are readily available, tied into four portions with ribbon or string. A 1lb (450g) pack will feed four to six people comfortably.

Other vegetables, such as red and yellow peppers and corgettes, can be added or substituted for any of the vegetables given below. For the seafood, try to include peeled shrimps, clams, cockles or squid. When pushed we have used 4oz (110g) bottled Italian seafood in oil or brine.

SERVES 4–6

1 large carrot, peeled

4oz (110g) button mushrooms, wiped

2 leeks or onions, trimmed

3 tablespoons oil

1 clove garlic, peeled and crushed

4 rashers of streaky bacon, cut into thin strips

4oz (110g) white cabbage, finely shredded

1 teaspoon salt

½ teaspoon white pepper

1 tablespoon soy sauce

3 tablespoons chicken stock or water

4oz (110g) seafood (any variety or a mixture of several types)

2 tablespoons sherry

½ teaspoon *Sambol Ulek* (p. 28, optional)

1 × 1lb (450g) packet rice sticks (*meehoon*) soaked and drained (see above)

½ teaspoon sesame seed oil (optional)

1. Cut the carrot, mushrooms and leeks or onions into julienne or batons approximately 1 inch (2.5cm) in length.

2. Heat the oil in a wok and stir-fry the onions or leeks and garlic for 2 minutes. Add the bacon, carrot sticks and cabbage and fry for 2 minutes more.

3. Add all the rest of the ingredients except the noodles and sesame oil. Mix well.

4. Finally add the noodles and fry for about 3 minutes or until most of the liquid has been absorbed by the noodles.

5. Mix in the sesame seed oil, if using, and serve.

VARIATION

✦ Beat 2 eggs with 1 tablespoon water and ½ teaspoon salt. Use 2 tablespoons at once in a non-stick frying pan to make 2 very thin omelettes. Turn over and, when cooked, stack on a plate. Repeat until all the egg mixture has been used up. Roll each omelette into a cigar shape, cut into thin shreds and use to garnish the *meehoon*.

Fried crispy rice sticks

This Thai speciality is a very easy-to-make all-in-one dish for family and friends.

SERVES 4

1 pint (570ml) oil for deep-frying

8oz (225g) rice sticks (*meehoon*)

1 onion, peeled and finely chopped

2 cloves garlic, peeled and finely chopped

4oz (110g) fillet of pork, sliced into thin strips

4oz (110g) breast of chicken, sliced into thin strips

4oz (110g) fresh whole prawns

12oz (350g) bean sprouts

1 bunch or about 6 large spring onions, washed, trimmed and chopped

1 tablespoon lemon juice

1 tablespoon soy sauce

2 tablespoons fish sauce

2 tablespoons malt vinegar

1. Heat the oil in a wok. When very hot put small handfuls of rice sticks in and fry until crisp. Remove with a metal spatula and drain on paper towels. Fry all the noodles this way.

2. Carefully pour all but 4 tablespoons of the oil into a metal container and use for some other purpose.

3. Put the wok back on the heat, and stir-fry the onion and garlic in the 4 tablespoons of oil until golden brown. Add the pork, chicken and prawns and cook until the flesh just turns opaque (about 3 minutes).

4. Add all the remaining ingredients except the deep-fried noodles. Mix well.

5. Finally, toss in the noodles, stir and serve.

VARIATION

✦ Garnish with chopped coriander leaves and a sprinkling of *Balichaw* (p. 26).

LAKSA

MALAYSIAN CURRIED SOUP

❀

THIS savoury spicy noodle dish is full of fish, prawns and seafood in a coconut sauce and is a national dish. We have amended it slightly but all the flavours echo *laksa* as we remember it. *Laksa* is a cross between a soup and a noodle dish. A bowlful makes a satisfying main course.

SERVES 4–6

8oz (225g) rice vermicelli
½ teaspoon salt
½ teaspoon ground black pepper
8oz (225g) boneless white fish fillets, skinned
2 tablespoons flour, to roll fish balls
2oz (50g) fresh or tinned crab meat
8oz (225g) peeled shrimps or prawns
6oz (175g) bean sprouts

4 spring onions, washed, trimmed and chopped
1 whole cucumber, finely sliced
1 teaspoon shrimp paste (*blachan*), mixed to a paste with 1 teaspoon water
2oz (50g) creamed coconut
1 teaspoon oil
2 kaffir lime leaves (optional)

1. Soak the vermicelli in boiling water for 10 minutes, drain and set aside.

2. Put the salt, pepper and fish into a liquidiser and whizz until it forms a paste. Flour your hands and shape the paste into 1 inch (2.5cm) balls.

3. Bring 2 pints (1 litre) water to the boil in a pan, carefully lower the fish balls into it and simmer for 2 minutes. Remove with a slotted spoon.

4. Add all the remaining ingredients to the water in the pan and bring to the boil. Stir carefully to mix the flavours, then simmer for 3–4 minutes.

5. Return the fish balls to the soup and serve in deep bowls with lime wedges and a small dish of *Sambol Ulek* (p. 28).

VARIATION

✦ We have made our own '*Laksa*' with plain boiled spaghetti, leftover beef, lamb or chicken curry, and extra water. As long as the bean sprouts and cucumber are included, and the dish is spiced with coconut milk and *blachan* and served with lime wedges, it makes a tolerable substitute and is a great way to use up leftovers.

SPICY NOODLES
WITH BARBECUED MEAT & SPINACH

A WONDERFUL way of using up any leftover Char Sui Pork (p. 98) or Satay (p. 95) meat, this supper dish is quick and easy to prepare and best served freshly made.

SERVES 4–6

1lb (450g) egg noodles

2 tablespoons oil

1 clove garlic, peeled and crushed

8oz (250g) cooked meat, cut into small cubes

8oz (250g) spinach, washed and cut into strips

½ teaspoon ground coriander

½ teaspoon ground cumin

½ teaspoon salt

1 small red chilli, chopped

1 tablespoon soy sauce

1 tablespoon cornflour, mixed with 2 tablespoons sherry

1. Cook the noodles in plenty of boiling water. Drain and keep to one side.

2. Heat the oil in a wok and, when smoking, add the garlic. Stir-fry for a few seconds, then add the meat, spinach, coriander, cumin and salt. Stir-fry for 2 minutes.

3. Add the noodles, chilli and soy sauce, and then the cornflour mixture.

4. Stir constantly until the sauce thickens.

VARIATIONS

✦ If you prefer a hotter dish, add ½–1 teaspoon *Sambol Ulek* (p. 28).

✦ We sometimes stir in 2 teaspoons crunchy peanut butter to give a subtle nutty undertone and a more Indonesian flavour. Cream the peanut butter with the cornflour and sherry mixture and add at step 3.

Meat

Unlike most Westerners, South-East Asian, Oriental and Sri Lankan people tend to eat only very small amounts of protein. Instead, we enjoy many different types of dishes – rice, flour products, vegetables, seafood or fish and meat – at one meal.

The eating patterns of this part of the world largely reflect the many different religions found here. The Christians and Chinese have few taboos and eat practically anything; Muslims will not eat pork; Hindus abhor beef.

Cooking styles also vary – from braising or stewing (curries and Chinese 'red' cooking in soy sauce rely on these methods) to very quick stir-frying, grilling and barbecuing. The cooking style is partly determined by the cut of meat – expensive tender cuts, such as frying steak, or fillet of lamb or pork, are ideal for fast cooking. By contrast, meat from parts of the animal which have to work harder (including the legs, haunches and neck) are muscular and need slow cooking to tenderise the flesh. These are the cheaper joints, marked stewing or braising meat.

Most of our recipes can be adapted to use any other protein whether meat or fish.

One ingredient common to curries all over this region is a small quantity (about a teaspoon) of either dried salted prawns/shrimps or maldive fish. Believe us, the fishy taste is not apparent, but the curries have a 'note' or depth when cooked this way which is most pleasant, and so unlike the curries you may be used to eating.

SIMPLE MALAY BEEF SATAY

Dad lived in Malaysia for the first 30-odd years of his life and it was here that he met and wooed our mother Koh Yue Woon, whose stage name was Anna Koh. Not surprisingly the cuisines of Malaysia and Singapore are very important to our family. We naturally gravitate to the Asian/Chinese sweet/hot/sour/spicy flavours of this region. Satay – small chunks of meat soaked in a spicy marinade and then grilled, broiled or barbecued on sticks – is definitely one of our favourites. Satay means 'three' in a Malaysian dialect – traditionally only three pieces of meat were skewered on each stick.

Bamboo sticks are available from Chinese food shops but you can use metal skewers instead. If using bamboo sticks, soak them for at least a couple of hours beforehand so they don't burn. A little kitchen foil wrapped around the ends helps prevent this and looks attractive too.

SERVES 6

1½lb (700g) good-quality steak

1 tablespoon jaggery (palm sugar) or dark brown sugar

2 teaspoons each ground turmeric, cumin and coriander

1½ teaspoons salt

1 teaspoon chilli powder

1 teaspoon lime or lemon juice

2 tablespoons coconut powder or a 2oz (50g) block coconut cream mixed with 1–2 tablespoons very hot water

50 bamboo skewers, soaked in water

1. Cut the beef into ½ inch (1cm) cubes.

2. Mix all the ingredients in a large bowl, add the beef and marinate for at least 2 hours. Overnight is best.

3. Thread the beef cubes onto skewers.

4. Preheat the grill to high and cook the meat, basting with leftover marinade and turning the sticks frequently, or place on a barbecue. The sticks are done when the beef is brown and the delicious smells make your guests start chewing the carpet in anticipation.

5. Serve with Compressed Rice Cakes (p. 71), Satay Sauce (p. 32) and chilli sauce. We serve fresh salads as well, and a bowl of cucumber batons (p. 69).

VARIATION

✦ **Chicken satay** is very good too. Use breast meat cut into long strips and thread each strip onto a skewer. Brush with oil before grilling.

BEEF SMOORE
SRI LANKAN BRAISED BEEF IN A SPICY COCONUT SAUCE

WE REALLY love this dish – the gravy is rich and savoury, redolent of spices and coconut milk. *Smoore* makes an unusual buffet dish which benefits from being made a few days in advance. We usually make it at Christmas when palates are jaded by the everlasting turkey – Boxing Day is certainly enlivened by this recipe. Cut the meat into very thin pieces and serve with boiled rice, salads and *Seeni Sambol* (p. 37).

Try to get stewing beef which has a fringe of fat, and is marbled with it too. The fat keeps the meat from drying out and makes for succulent eating.

SERVES 6–8 *as a main dish, or 15 as part of a buffet*

a 3lb (1.5kg) piece of stewing beef
2 medium onions, peeled and chopped
5 cloves garlic, peeled and crushed
1 tablespoon chopped fresh ginger
1 stick of cinnamon
2 cloves
2 star anise
12 curry leaves (optional)
1 stalk of lemon grass (or the grated rind of
  1 lemon)
3 tablespoons malt vinegar
1 tablespoon chilli powder

2 teaspoons ground turmeric
1 tablespoon ground cumin
2 teaspoons ground mixed spice
2 teaspoons salt
2 teaspoons freshly ground black pepper
a 2oz (50g) block tamarind dissolved in
  1 pint (570ml) hot water, *or* the juice of
  3 lemons and 1 teaspoon brown sugar
½ teaspoon fenugreek seeds (optional)
1 × 7oz (200g) block coconut cream
3 tablespoons ghee or coconut oil

1. Use a long metal skewer and stab the meat all over, very deeply. This is very therapeutic in the stressful days during the run up to Christmas!

2. Put all the ingredients, except the coconut cream and ghee or oil, in a pan and cook over a medium heat, covered, for 1–1½ hours or until the meat is tender but not falling apart. Add extra water if needed to stop it sticking to the bottom of the pan.

3. Add the coconut cream and cook, uncovered, over a high heat for another 10 minutes or until most of the liquid has reduced. Keep turning the meat and stirring the bottom so the sauce does not catch. It should be the consistency of thick jam. Pick out and discard the largest pieces of spices.

4. Remove the meat. Put the oil in a wok and heat. When smoking, carefully put the meat in (be careful of splattering fat) and fry on all sides until a rich brown. Add the sauce and heat through.

VARIATION
✦ Boneless lamb and pork joints are equally good for this dish. Select cuts marbled with fat to keep the meat moist.

Beef rendang

RENDANG is a hot, spicy, aromatic and dry dish and variations on it pop up in Indonesia, Malaysia, Singapore and Bali. We invented a special instant *rendang* curry mix which we sell to restaurants. It was one of the top three recipes we started our mail order business with and is still a firm family favourite.

Rendang can be kept in the refrigerator for up to four days. The flavours develop and mature so it is ideal for parties when you want to prepare as much in advance as possible. Serve with freshly boiled rice, Gado Gado (p. 142) and Satay Sauce (p. 32).

SERVES 4–6

1 tablespoon ground coriander
1 tablespoon ground cumin
1 teaspoon salt
1 teaspoon ground turmeric
1 teaspoon chilli powder
2 teaspoons jaggery (palm sugar) or dark brown sugar
3oz (75g) coconut powder or block of creamed coconut mixed with a little hot water
¼ teaspoon ground black pepper

½oz (14g) tamarind juice (a ½ oz/14g block mixed with 3 tablespoons hot water and sieved)
1 large onion, peeled and cut into chunks
3 cloves garlic, peeled and crushed
1 teaspoon ginger, peeled and crushed
3 cardamom pods, crushed
1 stalk of lemon grass, cut into small pieces
1 tablespoon oil
1lb (450g) good-quality steak, cut into thin strips

1. Put all the ingredients, except the oil and meat, into a liquidiser with 9fl oz (250ml) water, and blend to an almost smooth liquid paste.

2. Heat the oil in a pan and brown the meat strips. Add the prepared paste and bring to the boil.

3. Reduce the heat and cook until all the water has evaporated and the meat begins to fry. Keep stirring to prevent the meat catching and burning.

VARIATION
✦ Lamb and pork are also good made into *rendang*. Choose tender cuts.

CHAR SUI PORK
ROAST OR BARBECUED CHINESE PORK

A CLASSIC, very easy-to-make but beautiful dish, with its dark outside rim surrounding a pale juicy centre. We cut the pork diagonally into wafer-thin slices to show as much of the contrasting colour as possible. You may be able to track down Chinese red, yellow and orange food dyes. The authentic colouring is red – add only ¼ teaspoon of the dye to the marinade and take great care, as the powder stains fingers and kitchen counters. It does contain chemical colourants, so we tend to use it only on very special occasions or not at all.

Char Sui pork or lamb fillet is delicious cooked on the barbecue, too. Choose cuts with some fat on them to keep the meat moist and succulent.

SERVES 4 *as a main meal, or 8 as part of a buffet*

5fl oz (150ml) soy sauce
3 tablespoons tomato ketchup
1 teaspoon brown sugar
3 tablespoons hoi sin sauce
2 cloves garlic, peeled and crushed

1 tablespoon ginger wine or sweet sherry
1 teaspoon salt
2lb (1kg) loin or shoulder of pork, cut into
   3 inch (7.5cm) long strips

1. Mix all the ingredients in a large bowl and marinate the meat for at least 4 hours or overnight. Turn it over a couple of times so the liquid has a chance to soak in.

2. Preheat the oven to 220°C/425°F/Gas Mark 7. Place the pork strips in the oven on a grill rack or oven rack with a foil-lined pan underneath to catch the drips.

3. Roast for 15 minutes, then lower the heat to 180°C/350°F/Gas Mark 4 and cook for a further 10–15 minutes, or until cooked through but still very moist and succulent in the middle. Ovens vary in temperature so keep an eye on this and adjust the timing according to your own oven.

4. Brush the meat with the marinade frequently and turn over so all sides get a baked-on coating of sauce.

5. Remove from the oven, slice and serve with freshly boiled rice, cucumber batons (p. 69) and carrot sticks, a vegetable stir-fry, and a range of dips including *Nam Prik* (p. 27).

VARIATIONS

✦ Hoi sin sauce is widely available and does add a special flavour. If you cannot get hold of it, substitute the same quantity of honey, 1 teaspoon lemon juice and 1 teaspoon ground cinnamon.

✦ We have also used lamb ribs for this dish very successfully. Remove as much fat as possible and only use the meaty parts of a breast of lamb.

TIGER LILY SWEET & SOUR PORK RIBS

WHAT A glorious animal a pig is. We utilise every part of it except the squeak. It is particularly popular in China and the countries that border the Pacific Rim because its tender meat is ideal for quick stir-frying. It is also easy to keep and you often see pigs rooting around villages alongside dogs. Many countries, like Malaysia and Indonesia, are Muslim and naturally pork is not eaten there. However, the Christians and Chinese have adapted local recipes to suit their favourite meat.

American spare ribs, or Chinese ribs, come from the belly of the pig. We usually try to buy the whole belly cut – the meaty ribs we cook in sweet and sour sauce, the thicker lean flank is good for turning into barbecued *Char Sui* (p. 98) strips, while the fattier meat and skin make excellent sweet and sour pork. Mother used to cut the fat and skin into small pieces, fry them slowly in a wok to crisp, then drain off the excess oil to use for frying or roasting potatoes. The crispy skin left behind would be used to add a delicious crunchy texture to stir-fried dishes.

For this recipe, ask your butcher to cut the ribs into manageable portions, or use a cleaver yourself.

SERVES 3–4

1 quantity Tiger Lily's Special Sweet & Sour Sauce (p. 30)	2lb (900g) spare ribs, cut into bite-sized pieces
2 tablespoons soy sauce	1 teaspoon oil (sesame if possible)

1. Preheat the oven to 200°C/400°F/Gas Mark 6.

2. Mix the sweet and sour sauce with the soy sauce in a large bowl and marinate the ribs for at least 4 hours or overnight.

3. Place the ribs in a shallow baking tray, brush with a little oil, then cook for about 20 minutes.

4. Reduce the heat to 180°C/350°F/Gas Mark 4 and cook for an additional 30 minutes. Turn the ribs over with tongs a few times during cooking, and baste with leftover marinade.

5. Serve hot with boiled rice.

BURMESE PORK CURRY WITH STRAW MUSHROOMS

A DRY SPICY curry, rich and dark but with an interesting extra – little straw mushrooms.

SERVES 4–6

1lb (450g) boneless shoulder of pork, not too lean, cut into 2 inch (5cm) cubes

½ teaspoon chilli powder

½ teaspoon ground turmeric

1 teaspoon salt

2 medium onions, peeled and chopped

1 stalk of lemon grass, crushed, or the rind and juice of 1 lemon

2 cloves garlic, peeled and chopped

1 teaspoon sliced chopped galangal or ginger, peeled and cut into very thin shreds

2 small fresh red or green chillies, chopped

¼ teaspoon *blachan* (shrimp paste) or ½ teaspoon dried shrimps

2 tablespoons tamarind juice (1oz (25g) tamarind mixed with 1 tablespoon water and sieved)

2 tablespoons oil

12oz (350g) tinned straw mushrooms, drained

1 teaspoon ground dried prawns (optional)

1. Prick the meat all over with a skewer, put it in a bowl and mix with the dry spices and salt. Put aside to marinate for about 2 hours.

2. Put the onions, lemon grass, garlic, galangal or ginger, chillies, *blachan* or dried shrimps and tamarind juice into a liquidiser and process to a purée.

3. Heat the oil in a pan and add the purée. Cook, stirring constantly, until the liquid evaporates, the mixture begins to fry, and the oil starts to separate out.

4. Add the pork and fry in its own juice for 15–20 minutes or until the meat is cooked. Keep stirring and add a little water to prevent it burning, if necessary.

5. Stir in the straw mushrooms, and ground dried prawns if using, simmer for 5 minutes and serve.

VARIATION

◆ The soft, creamy straw mushrooms make a pleasant contrast to the spicy meat. If they are not available you can substitute tinned champignons. Sprinkle a few chopped coriander leaves over the dish before serving if you wish but go easy – it is quite a strong herb and you do not want to swamp the flavour.

CHINESE STIR-FRIED LAMB WITH ONIONS

❀

THIS IS a very delicious, quick and easy family favourite.

SERVES 4

12oz (350g) lamb fillet, sliced very thinly across the grain
1 teaspoon sugar
1 teaspoon salt
1 tablespoon soy sauce
1 tablespoon cornflour

2 tablespoons vegetable oil
1 clove garlic, peeled and crushed
1 teaspoon grated ginger
2 medium onions, peeled and sliced
1 teaspoon crushed black peppercorns
½ teaspoon sesame oil

1. Put the lamb in a bowl and mix with the sugar, salt, soy sauce and cornflour.

2. Heat the vegetable oil in a wok until it smokes. Add the garlic and ginger and stir for a few seconds just to flavour the oil.

3. Add the onions and crushed peppercorns and stir until the onions are just cooked. Remove from the heat and set aside.

4. Heat the sesame oil in the wok (do not bring to a smoking heat, as this destroys some of the delicate flavour), add the meat and stir-fry for 3 minutes or until the lamb is no longer pink. Take care not to overcook.

5. Add the onions and 2 tablespoons water and stir until the sauce becomes thick and glossy.

Sri Lankan Lamb & Spinach Curry

WE LOVE this mixture of spinach and lamb – the stunning contrast of dark meat, rich creamy sauce and green leaves makes it a feast for the eyes as well as the tastebuds. It is simplicity itself to cook if you have some ready-prepared Sri Lankan Curry Sauce in the fridge or freezer.

SERVES 4

5 tablespoons oil

1lb (450g) shoulder of lamb, cut into 1 inch (2.5cm) cubes

¼ quantity Sri Lankan Curry Sauce (p. 25)

1 teaspoon salt

½–1 teaspoon chilli powder (according to taste)

1½ teaspoons Garam Masala (p. 21)

1 teaspoon maldive fish or ground dried prawns

1lb (450g) canned or frozen puréed spinach

2 teaspoons finely chopped coriander leaves

1. Heat the oil in a large saucepan, add the lamb and fry until just browned (about 5 minutes).

2. Add the curry sauce, 11fl oz (300ml) water and the rest of the ingredients, except the spinach and coriander leaves. Bring to the boil, then lower the heat and simmer for about 15 minutes or until the curry thickens. Stir constantly to prevent burning.

3. Add the spinach and stir gently to heat through for a few minutes only.

4. Stir in the chopped coriander leaves just before serving.

VARIATION

✦ Add a finely chopped green chilli and a swirl (about 2 tablespoons) of thick yoghurt with the coriander leaves at step 4.

LAMB KEBABS IN CORIANDER AND MINT, WITH LEMON YOGHURT

USE A boned shoulder or leg of lamb for this sensational dish which makes a superb alternative to steak and hamburgers for summer barbecues. Prepare the kebabs the day before and keep refrigerated, covered in clingfilm. The mint and coriander flavours complement the sweet tender lamb perfectly, though boneless pork also works well.

SERVES 4

1lb (450g) boneless lamb, cut into 1 inch (2.5cm) cubes
2 teaspoons mint sauce
1 tablespoon freshly chopped mint
1½ teaspoons salt
1 teaspoon freshly ground black pepper
1 teaspoon ground coriander

1 tablespoon lemon juice
11fl oz (300ml) thick low-fat yoghurt
1 tablespoon oil
2 tablespoons melted butter, to brush kebabs
2 lemons (choose thin-skinned ones)

1. Start the night before. Put the meat in a bowl with 1 teaspoon of the mint sauce, 1 teaspoon of the chopped fresh mint, the salt, pepper and coriander, 1 teaspoon of the lemon juice, 2 tablespoons of yoghurt, and the oil. Mix well and cover with clingfilm. Store in the refrigerator overnight.

2. Thread the meat on bamboo sticks (soaked in water for 30 minutes so they do not burn) or on metal skewers.

3. Mix the melted butter with the rest of the lemon juice and use to baste the kebabs.

4. Barbecue or cook under a preheated grill until cooked through (about 30 minutes), brushing with butter and lemon juice, and turning over halfway through the cooking time.

5. Meanwhile wash the lemons and cut one into wedges for decoration. Cut the other lemon into pieces and remove as many seeds as you can. Put the de-seeded lemon into a food processor and process until finely chopped.

6. Put the chopped lemon into a bowl and mix with the remaining mint, mint sauce and yoghurt.

7. Serve the kebabs on a large platter decorated with fresh mint leaves and lemon wedges, rice or Quick and Easy Naan Bread (p. 82). Accompany with the lemon yoghurt and *Sambol Ulek* (p. 28) or one of the chilli sauces.

MONGOLIAN STEAM BOAT OR HOT POT

A GREAT speciality of the north of China is Mongolian Hot Pot, or Steam Boat. This all-in-one dish is made at the dinner table in a metal pan which looks like a miniature stove, with a chimney running through it. Coals are lit in the bottom to keep the flavoured stock in the pan at a rolling boil. Guests sit around the pot with a supply of raw prawns, scallops, fish, squid, chicken, lamb, beef, *pak choi* (Chinese cabbage), bean sprouts, cellophane noodles and spring onions handy. They use chopsticks to drop in whatever meat or vegetables they fancy and each has a small metal basket on a long handle to fish out the cooked ingredients, dip them in a range of sauces and eat them immediately.

The stock becomes richer and more flavoursome as the evening progresses. Finally, when all the meat and vegetables are gone, the noodles are added and eaten with some of the soup.

Try our simplified version of this great dish, using lamb. As Steam Boat involves almost instant cooking, if you use beef you need to use the best, most tender cuts. And it is not necessary to own a steam boat to enjoy this dish. A saucepan over a high heat will do.

SERVES 4

8oz (225g) boneless lamb

1½ pints (850ml) Homemade Chicken Stock (p. 33) or 2 Knorr chicken stock cubes dissolved in the same quantity of boiling water

½ teaspoon salt (optional)

2oz (50g) water chestnuts, sliced

4oz (110g) spinach, washed and torn into large pieces

4oz (110g) bamboo shoots, cut into shreds

4oz (110g) bean sprouts, washed

4oz (110g) cellophane noodles, cut with scissors into 2 inch (5cm) pieces, soaked in hot water for 30 minutes before use, then drained

1. Cut the lamb into paper-thin 1 inch (2.5cm) squares.

2. Put the stock in a pan and bring to the boil. Taste and add the salt only if necessary.

3. Drop the ingredients in and boil for 3 minutes only or until the lamb loses its pinkness. Take care not to overcook.

4. Serve in bowls with chopsticks and soup spoons, with a selection of sauces, including Vietnamese Fish Sauce (p. 29) and *Sambol Ulek* (p. 28).

Poultry

Poor old chickens are the most unfortunate creatures in the world. Everyone (other than vegetarians) enjoys eating them and their eggs, and every village in South-East Asia has flocks of colourful fowl scratching in the dust and scattering, squawking and complaining, at the approach of cars or little children who find endless pleasure in chasing them! Our chickens are yellow and full of flavour when cooked but tend to be tougher than the large, flabby, tender but tasteless white fowl available in the West. We always go for a boiling fowl for curries (utterly delicious) and a free-range or corn-fed bird for quick cooking or roasting.

Incidentally, do not throw away the fat that you find in the body cavity or under the breast in a roasting or boiling chicken. Instead, cut the fat into small pieces and slowly heat it in a pan until it melts. This fat can be kept in a refrigerator for up to three weeks. It makes excellent roast potatoes and also adds a special flavour to stir-fried dishes.

When we were young, Mother used to keep chickens and we once – aged four and six – broke our hearts and cried with remorse after innocently drowning half a dozen fluffy yellow chicks in the bath. We thought they needed the yolk cleaned off them, but our podgy little hands squeezed them so tightly they had no chance of survival. The product of strict Methodist grandparents, we insisted they were given proper funerals with tiny flower garlands and hymns, and grieved for quite some time.

Ducks are very popular in China and racks upon racks of the shiny mahogany brown fowl are seen hanging in restaurant windows in the Orient, tempting passers-by with their wonderful aroma. One of our favourite meals is duck rice – a plate of steaming white rice topped with pieces of barbecued duck, plain steamed *pak choi* or some other green vegetable, and soy sauce.

The triumphant crow of a cock, followed by the raucous cawing of crows, used to wake us each morning, whether in town, city or village. In Hong Kong, where space is at a premium, people even keep chickens in high-rise flats!

EASY SWEET & SOUR CHICKEN WITH BAMBOO SHOOTS & CASHEW NUTS

THIS IS a recipe for those 'do I really have to cook?' days. If you are nifty with a knife and a tin-opener you can have this on the table within 10 minutes. It is perfect if you assemble all the ingredients the night before, and leave them in the fridge, covered with clingfilm. Then, after a hard day at the office, a quick 'zap' in the wok produces instant Oriental magic.

SERVES 3–4

½ teaspoon salt

2 teaspoons cornflour

2 large chicken breasts, weighing approximately 1lb (450g), sliced into thin strips

2 tablespoons oil

2oz (50g) canned bamboo shoots

1 red or green pepper, washed, with seeds and pith removed, cut into 1 inch (2.5cm) squares

1 small onion, peeled and finely sliced

1 clove garlic, peeled and crushed

a 1½ inch (4cm) piece of fresh ginger, peeled and crushed

½ quantity Tiger Lily's Special Sweet & Sour Sauce (p. 30) *or* 1 tablespoon hoi sin sauce, 1 tablespoon tomato ketchup and 1 teaspoon soy sauce

1 tablespoon ginger wine or sweet sherry

4oz (110g) roasted salted cashew nuts

1. Mix the salt and cornflour together, add the chicken and mix together.

2. Heat a wok and add the oil. When it begins to smoke add the chicken and stir-fry for 3 minutes. Remove the chicken with a slotted spoon, drain on paper towels and keep warm.

3. Put the rest of the ingredients in the wok, except the sweet and sour sauce (or alternative seasonings), the ginger wine or sherry and the cashew nuts. Stir-fry for about 3 minutes, then add the cooked chicken, sweet and sour sauce (or alternative seasonings), ginger wine or sherry, and heat through.

4. Stir in the cashew nuts and serve with boiled rice.

VARIATION

✦ Add a handful of chopped water chestnuts, fresh bean sprouts or sticks of cucumber to the wok with the sherry at step 3. These should all stay crisp and only be lightly stir-fried for not more than 2 minutes.

CHICKEN BATONS

A FUN STARTER but good for party buffets too. Wrap a small piece of kitchen foil around the end of the bone to make it less messy to pick up. Chicken wings are cheap and easily available. Choose small ones for this recipe. They are perfect for a mouthful, and you can prepare them a day in advance. All you need is a chopping board and a sharp knife.

Make at least twice as many as you would expect any normal person to eat – they disappear like magic.

MAKES 20–24; *enough for 4–6 as a starter or 10–15 as part of a buffet*

2lb (1kg) chicken wings	2 eggs
8oz (225g) self-raising flour	1 teaspoon sesame oil
4oz (110g) cornflour	salt and pepper
½ teaspoon salt	1¾ pints (1 litre) oil, for deep-frying

1. Cut the wing into 3 pieces at the joints (see opposite). Discard the wing tips or use them to make Homemade Chicken Stock (p. 33).

2. Take the 2 remaining portions and, using a knife, loosen the meat from the bone and pull it down to the end of the joint. When you get to the end, pull it right over the bone and tuck in to form a ball. Imagine the bone is your leg and you are rolling a stocking down it, and bunching it around your foot! It should end up looking like a mini toffee apple. (See opposite.)

3. The joint nearest the wing tip has 2 bones – work one bone free, cut through the tendon and discard the bone. You will end up with a plateful of what looks like mini drum batons.

4. To make the batter, put the flour, cornflour and ½ teaspoon salt in a mixing bowl with the eggs and sesame oil. Add just under 12fl oz (350ml) water and beat together until it becomes a thick cream.

5. Salt and pepper the chicken batons, then dip them into the batter. Shake off the excess.

6. Heat the cooking oil in a wok or deep-fryer until it begins to smoke, then drop in the batons and fry until cooked through or for about 5–8 minutes, depending on the size of the 'balls'. Cook in 2–3 batches, depending on the size of your wok. Drain on paper towels, and serve with Tiger Lily's Special Sweet & Sour Sauce (p. 30), Satay Sauce (p. 32) or any chilli sauce.

VARIATION

◆ Place 4oz (110g) lightly toasted sesame seeds in a bowl beside the sauces. Guests take a baton, dip it in the sauce of their choice and then in the sesame seeds before eating.

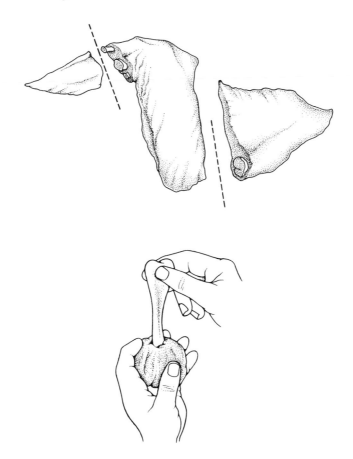

BARBECUED DUCK

WE TRAVELLED extensively around the world when we were young, rarely staying longer than two or three years in any one spot. We took few possessions with us but one that we have always had, which has ended up in Rani's kitchen, is a dark stone pestle and mortar from Thailand.

When we were posted to England in 1955 our servants and cook refused to accompany us – they had heard about the cold, wet English weather and were not prepared to leave beautiful tropical Sri Lanka!

Mum was a hopeless cook. Having always been surrounded by domestic help, she couldn't even boil rice let alone an egg. In the early days we shared a flat with a family in Bromley until we found permanent accommodation, and their mother had to give Mum a hand or we would have starved.

After a month of unrelieved bacon and mashed potato pie and English roasts we all rebelled and Mum was forced to invent something. Out came the pestle and mortar, and ginger and garlic were pounded with soy sauce, sugar, vinegar and sherry until they formed a paste, which was then rubbed on just about anything – from chops to chicken – before roasting.

Amazingly, this mix has survived to this day, although we are now more inclined to save work and use a blender or liquidiser to blend the ingredients. You can store the sauce in the fridge in an airtight container for up to 4 days.

SERVES 4–6; *enough for a 3lb 4oz (1.5kg) duck or chicken,*
2lb (900g) Chinese spare ribs, or 1 large fish

2 cloves garlic, peeled
4 slices fresh ginger, peeled
1 tablespoon soy sauce
1 tablespoon honey or sugar

1 dessertspoon malt vinegar
1 tablespoon sweet sherry
3 teaspoons salt

1. Pound the garlic and ginger in a mortar and pestle, then add the liquid ingredients and salt to make a sauce. Or put all the ingredients in a blender or liquidiser and blend until completely smooth. It can be used as a rub, a marinade, or in stir-fries.

2. For barbecued duck, leave the duck to marinate in the sauce for at least 4 hours or overnight, turning frequently to let the flavours sink in.

3. Preheat the oven to 190°C/375°F/Gas Mark 5. Put the bird on its breast and roast for 1 hour, basting occasionally with the marinade and juices in the pan.

4. Reduce the temperature to 150°C/300°F/Gas Mark 2, turn the bird on to its back and cook for another 45 minutes. Baste again.

5. If needed, add 1 tablespoon water to the pan to stop the juices burning. Plunge a skewer into the bird between the thigh and body (where the meat is thickest). If the juice runs clear the duck is done; if not, cook until it does run clear. The skin should be a deep mahogany colour. If not, turn the temperature up to 190°C/375°F/Gas Mark 5 and roast until it browns.

VARIATIONS

✦ Try adding one or some of the following ingredients but also think up some of your own:

2 small fresh green chillies, chopped

1 tablespoon peanut butter

1 tablespoon ginger wine instead of the sherry

2 slices galangal instead of the ginger

1 tablespoon fresh coriander leaves

PAPER-WRAPPED CHICKEN & MANGE TOUT

THIS NEXT recipe must be the only low-calorie, healthy, deep-fried one you will ever come across. It looks very spectacular and is ideal for entertaining as it can be prepared the day before, then fried just before serving. All the ingredients must be at their absolute freshest. Guests open the individual packets at the table so none of the aroma is lost. Wonderful!

MAKES 20–24 *packets; enough for 4–6*

3 spring onions, washed, trimmed and finely shredded, or a 2 inch (5cm) piece of galangal, peeled and cut into very thin batons or juliennes
2 tablespoons soy sauce
1 tablespoon rice wine or sweet sherry
1 teaspoon sugar
1 teaspoon hoi sin sauce
20–24 mange tout, weighing approximately 1½ oz (35g)
2 chicken breast fillets, weighing approximately 12oz (350g), cut into 20–24 pieces
2 teaspoons sesame oil
1½ pints (1 litre) oil, for deep-frying

1. Put the spring onions or galangal in a bowl with the soy sauce, rice wine or sherry, sugar, hoi sin sauce, mange tout and chicken and leave to marinate for 20 minutes.

2. Prepare 20–24 squares of 6 inch (15cm) waxed or greaseproof paper. Brush each piece of paper on one side with a little sesame oil. Put it on a flat surface, oiled side up, with a corner facing you. It should look like a diamond. Put a little spring onion or galangal, a piece of chicken, then a pea pod in the middle of the paper.

3. Bring up the bottom corner to cover the ingredients. Now fold over the right corner, then the left over the ingredients. Bring the top corner down towards you, then tuck it into the flap made by the folded corners. This is the same method used for Stuffed Spring Rolls (p. 50).

4. Heat the oil in a wok until it begins to smoke. Deep-fry the packages, a few at a time, for 2 minutes on each side. When all the packages are cooked bring the oil up to smoking point and re-fry in 2 batches for a further minute to reheat thoroughly. Drain on paper towels.

5. Place on a serving dish with a selection of chilli sauces and Vietnamese Fish Sauce (p. 29), providing an empty plate for the discarded papers. Guests open each package at the table and dunk the contents in the dipping sauce before eating.

VARIATION

♦ You can use the same method with whole giant fresh prawns, or fillets of good-quality white fish.

INDONESIAN GRILLED SPICY CHICKEN

THIS IS a delicious alternative to plain grilled chicken and is also very good for barbecues. A lovely buttery 'crust' develops on the surface of the chicken and it looks and smells mouthwatering. Eat this with rice, Quick and Easy Naan Bread (p. 82), Coconut Rotis (p. 76) or other Oriental/Asian dishes, or really surprise everyone by serving it with garlic bread, green salad and potato salad.

This is an ideal dish for a dinner party. You can prepare the chicken to step 5 and keep it cool for up to 6 hours before serving. Then finish the dish with step 6, and serve.

1 × 3lb 4oz (1.5kg) chicken	4oz (110g) block coconut cream, mixed
1 medium onion, peeled and chopped	with 6fl oz (175ml) hot water
3 cloves garlic, peeled and chopped	½ teaspoon ground black pepper
2 fresh red chillies, chopped	¼ teaspoon ground turmeric
1 teaspoon crushed fresh ginger	1½ teaspoons salt
1 stalk of lemon grass, crushed, or the	2 tablespoons melted butter or ghee
grated rind of 1 lemon	juice of 1 lemon

1. Cut the chicken in half lengthways. Make deep horizontal cuts in the flesh, rinse with clean water and dry with paper towels.

2. Put the onion, garlic, chillies, ginger and lemon grass or lemon rind in a liquidiser with 1 tablespoon water and blend to a paste. Add the coconut cream.

3. Mix the pepper, turmeric and salt together and rub over the chicken, going deep into the cuts.

4. Put the coconut mixture in a wok, bring slowly to the boil and add the chicken. Simmer for 20 minutes or until the water evaporates, turning the chicken once or twice.

5. Remove the chicken from the wok and keep to one side. Add the melted butter or ghee and the lemon juice to the wok.

6. When ready to serve, preheat a grill and brown the chicken on both sides, basting it with the spicy lemon-butter juices from the wok. This should take 10–15 minutes. Serve on a bed of watercress.

Eggs

BECAUSE ducks and hens are so widely raised in the Orient and South-East Asia, eggs are eaten frequently. Duck eggs are much prized, especially in China. But ducks are natural scavengers so their eggs require long, thorough cooking in order to kill any salmonella harboured in the rich, deep yellow yolks. They make wonderful Sweet and Sour Eggs (p. 115).

Hens' eggs are more readily available. The Chinese boil and cook them 'red' (in soy sauce) or stir beaten egg into a hot dish before taking it off the heat. This is just long enough for the egg to begin to coagulate and form thin threads, as in Egg Drop Soup (p. 60).

In Indonesia, Sri Lanka and other countries, omelettes are very popular. Sometimes they are flavoured with onions, chillies, sugar and spices or made more substantial with the addition of prawns or some other seafood.

One of our favourite breakfasts of all time is Mock Stringhoppers (p. 88), *Hodi* (p. 57), Coconut Sambol (p. 34) and plain omelette. A meal fit for a queen!

Sweet & Sour Eggs
WITH RED BRAISED PORK

EVERYONE loves sweet and sour pork but when we were children we would overlook the tender meat in this dish in favour of the dark brown savoury eggs, deeply slashed to show a streak of golden yolk. Eaten with rice, Mum's special carrot pickle, and quick fried beans this was as close to heaven as we could get.

Sweet and sour eggs make good party food. Simply follow the recipe but omit the pork. Carefully cut each egg into four segments and serve on a bed of shredded lettuce decorated with carved vegetable flowers (p. 123).

SERVES 6–8

1lb (450g) fatty pork (a belly cut is good, with the rind and fat)	6fl oz (175ml) soy sauce
8 hard-boiled eggs, shelled	1 tablespoon brown sugar
2 tablespoons oil	2 teaspoons salt
1 clove garlic, peeled and crushed	3 tablespoons malt vinegar
1 large onion, peeled and chopped	4 tablespoons sweet sherry
2 slices ginger, peeled and crushed	1 star anise (optional)

1. Cut the pork into 2 inch (5cm) cubes. Place each egg on a chopping board, holding it steady with one hand. Then, with a sharp knife, make deep vertical cuts all around the egg. Do not make the cuts too close to each other – all you are trying to do is let the rich sauce sink into the heart of the egg.

2. Heat the oil in a pan with a lid, then fry the garlic, onion and ginger until the onion softens. Add the pork and stir-fry until it begins to brown.

3. Put all the ingredients, except the eggs, into a deep pan with a lid. Add 4fl oz (110ml) water, cover and bring to the boil.

4. Carefully add the eggs, moving the pork chunks to one side so that all the eggs are under the sauce.

5. Simmer for about 1 hour. Very gently turn the eggs during cooking so that they are evenly covered with the sauce. It will gradually reduce and get very thick. When done, the meat becomes meltingly tender.

6. Place the meat and eggs in a dish, serve, and wait for the compliments.

EGG CURRY

A GREAT DISH — much under-rated we feel. In our version the eggs are rubbed with spices, then fried to seal the surface and finally cooked gently in a mild curry sauce.

SERVES 4–6

6 hard-boiled eggs, shelled

1 teaspoon ground turmeric

1–2 teaspoons salt

1 pint (570ml) oil, for deep-frying

1 medium onion, peeled and sliced

2 slices ginger, peeled and chopped

2 cloves garlic, peeled and crushed

1 teaspoon grated maldive fish or dried prawns (optional)

4 curry leaves (optional)

a 2 inch (5cm) piece *rampe* (pandanus leaf, optional)

¼ teaspoon ground cinnamon

½ teaspoon chilli powder

¼ teaspoon ground coriander

½ teaspoon ground cumin

½ teaspoon ground mixed spice

1 tomato, sliced

juice and rind of ½ lime

2oz (50g) block coconut cream

a pinch of Garam Masala (p. 21)

1. Prick the eggs all over with a metal skewer, to stop them bursting when they are fried. Rub with the turmeric and salt.

2. Heat the oil in a wok and deep-fry the eggs until they are a golden brown. Put the eggs in a dish and keep the oil on one side.

3. Put the onion, ginger and garlic in a blender or liquidiser with 5fl oz (150ml) water and blend to a paste.

4. Drain off all the oil from the wok except for 2 tablespoons and fry the onion paste, and maldive fish or dried prawns, curry leaves and *rampe* if using, until they begin to brown.

5. Add all the ingredients, except the eggs, coconut cream, and garam masala. Bring to the boil and simmer for 15 minutes or until the sauce begins to thicken.

6. Add the eggs, coconut cream and 11fl oz (300ml) water and simmer for a further 5–10 minutes. Stir in a pinch of Garam Masala to taste, and serve.

VARIATION

✦ Alternatively, follow steps 1 and 2, then add ¼ quantity Sri Lankan Curry Sauce (p. 25) to 2 tablespoons of the oil used to fry the eggs. Add the eggs, coconut cream, 11 fl oz (300ml) water and adjust the seasoning. Simmer for 10 minutes, and serve.

INDONESIAN SPICY OMELETTE

EVER SINCE someone hit on the notion of breaking an egg and frying it in oil, happy eaters around the world have tucked into variations on the omelette. The Spanish make a deep omelette with peppers and onions which is cut into wedges like a cake. Chinese omelettes are flavoured with mushrooms, crab meat and spring onions and usually fried in sesame oil. In South-East Asia the most popular ingredients are chillies and onions, as in this recipe from Indonesia.

SERVES 2–3

4 eggs

½ teaspoon salt

1 teaspoon soy sauce

½ teaspoon jaggery (palm sugar) or brown
    sugar

1 tablespoon oil

1 small onion, peeled and finely chopped

2 fresh green or red chillies, finely chopped

1. Beat the eggs until frothy, then add the salt, soy sauce and sugar.

2. Heat the oil in a frying pan. Fry the onion until brown, add the chillies and stir for a few seconds. Spread the mixture evenly over the pan.

3. Pour the eggs over the onion mixture. Cook over a low heat until the top begins to set and the bottom is brown.

4. Place on a warmed plate, and serve.

VARIATION

✦ 2oz (50g) crab meat or fresh peeled prawns can be added to the beaten eggs at step 1 to make a more substantial dish.

GOLDEN COIN EGGS

THIS RECIPE is so called because the folded eggs look like silk purses containing golden coins. Served with *Chok* or Chinese Watery Rice, this was one of our favourite childhood meals. Mother would get the servants to make this nourishing, easily digested Chinese speciality when we were convalescing from an illness.

SERVES 4

1 tablespoon oil	1 dessertspoon tomato ketchup
4 large eggs	½ teaspoon each sugar and salt
1 tablespoon soy sauce	1 teaspoon malt vinegar

1. Heat the oil in a frying pan.

2. Break the eggs into the pan as if making ordinary fried eggs, and cook over a medium heat. When almost set, use a spatula to gently fold each egg in half like a purse. Press gently on the edges to seal.

3. Add the rest of the ingredients to the pan and heat gently.

4. Before the eggs have set solid, carefully slide off onto bowls of thin *Chok* (p. 72).

VARIATION

✦ Serve with soy sauce, chopped spring onion and finely sliced *tung choi* (Chinese preserved vegetable) sprinkled over the top.

Fish & Seafood

FISH AND seafood are a major element in the staple diet of Thais, Malaysians, Sri Lankans and Indonesians. Anyone with a rod and pole can catch enough fish to feed themselves – the seas and rivers are teeming with a multitude of species which practically leap into the net or basket.

In Sri Lanka tourists flock to see the pole fishermen, who stand on tiny platforms built on wooden poles far out to sea. Silhouetted against the vivid crimson, emerald and vermilion hues of a tropical sunset they are wondrous to behold.

Also popular are the many types of shellfish found in South-East Asia. Abalone steaks make fine eating, as do the many clams and shellfish. As children, when we were being particularly obnoxious and driving the servants to despair, Mother would give us each a pail and send us to the beach to gather 'mutties' (small round clams). We would walk along the beach, feeling the sand with our toes and watching for the bubbles on the tide which showed where they were hiding. We would then pounce and fill our pails in a very short time (too quickly for Mother!). They would find their way into the pot for delicious soup noodles.

TIGER LILY TAMARIND FISH

BECAUSE we love eating so much, and were fortunate when young to have parents who could take us out regularly, we made firm friends with several families who ran Chinese restaurants in Sri Lanka. Mother's very good friends were the Suans who owned the Dragon Café in Colombo. All Chinese have a love of gambling and Mum would go to play Mah Jong with them. It is similar to gin rummy but the players use chunky painted tiles made of bone or plastic. We loved it when the tiles were turned face down at the end of the game and 'washed' (shuffled around the table). The noise was terrific as each tile clinked and clanked against its neighbours and we were sometimes allowed to join in.

The Suans were very generous, wonderful cooks and we first came across a whole baked fish at their Dragon Café. We enjoyed lavish banquets here and we once ate for so long (about four or five hours) that Chandra fell asleep in the middle of the noodles. Out like a light.

This recipe is spectacular although very easy to do. Wait for the 'Oooh!' from your guests when the parcel is opened at the table. Invest in a long oval dish (a turkey dish is ideal) so the fish does not flop over the sides!

2 small or one larger sea bass, trout or red snapper, gutted, but with the head left on

2 teaspoons dried tamarind, mixed with a little hot water and sieved

1 teaspoon salted black beans

1 teaspoon sugar

2 teaspoons soy sauce

1 teaspoon malt vinegar

½ teaspoon each crushed fresh ginger and garlic

4 spring onions, washed, trimmed and chopped

1. Slash the fish deeply on both sides, making parallel diagonal cuts. It looks even better if you heat a metal skewer and press it against the fish several times, going diagonally across the cuts. This 'branding' creates a very attractive diamond pattern.

2. Mix all the ingredients, except the spring onions, to a cream, then rub into the fish well, especially in between the cuts.

3. Place the fish in a large piece of foil, and sprinkle the chopped spring onions on top. Bring the sides up and form a loose tent at the top, turning the edges over twice to seal. Then bake in a preheated oven, at 220°C/425°F/Gas Mark 7, for about 20 minutes.

4. Bring to the table in the foil. When the 'tent' is opened a wonderful steam cloud of ginger and spices will waft up – very impressive!

VARIATION

✦ The fish can simply be placed on a plate and steamed for the same length of time.

SALT FISH CURRY

A LTHOUGH fresh fish is eaten so frequently in South-East Asia, to add interest and variety to our diet, we also eat salted fish – from small *harl masu* (tiny sprat-like fish), dried prawns and shrimps up to large cutlets from jack or king fish or tuna. We believe salted fish was introduced to Sri Lanka by the Portuguese, perhaps as a way of transporting the abundance of their South-East Asian territory back home. Walking around shops in Lisbon or the Algarve, we have seen identical slabs of salt cod to those found in Sri Lankan markets.

This is a dry curry, best served at a lukewarm temperature, with lots of boiled rice or Coconut Rotis (p. 76) and, of course, Coconut Sambol (p. 34) and Tomato, Cucumber and Onion Sambol (p. 36).

SERVES 3–4

8oz (250g) salt fish	2 cloves garlic, peeled and chopped
2 tablespoons oil	1½ teaspoons grated fresh ginger
1 large onion, peeled and chopped	3 curry leaves (optional)
1 tablespoon mustard seeds, ground with a little water	1 tablespoon malt vinegar
	1 teaspoon sugar
1 teaspoon chilli powder	1oz (25g) block coconut cream

1. Cut the salt fish into small pieces or shreds, heat the oil in a pan and fry the fish with the onion until both are crisp and beginning to brown.

2. Add the mustard seeds, chilli powder, garlic and ginger, and curry leaves if using, and stir gently for another 1–2 minutes.

3. Add the vinegar and sugar with 6 tablespoons water and simmer until all the liquid has gone. Crumble the coconut cream into the mixture and stir it in.

JEWEL FISH IN LEMON SAUCE

CHINA's Eastern Province's cuisine is similar to the Peking style of cooking. Shanghai is the major town here and, because of its coastal position, the local people tend to eat a lot of fish.

This recipe from Shanghai is for succulent fish in a light batter served with a deliciously different lemon sauce. If you wish, you could substitute chicken breast for the fish. Both are firm favourites of ours. Assemble the ingredients for the sauce, fish and batter before you start.

SERVES 4–6

For the sauce
4 tablespoons lemon juice
1 teaspoon grated lemon rind
2 teaspoons cornflour
10fl oz (275ml) Homemade Chicken Stock
 (p. 33) or ½ chicken stock cube dissolved
 in the same quantity of boiling water
2 spring onions, washed, trimmed and
 shredded
¼ teaspoon salt
1 tablespoon honey

For the fish
1lb (450g) white fish fillets, e.g. sole or
 cod, cut into bite-sized strips
1 tablespoon sherry or rice wine
1 teaspoon salt
3 tablespoons cornflour

For the batter
4oz (110g) self-raising flour
¼ teaspoon baking powder
1 egg
1 pint (570ml) oil, for deep-frying

1. Combine all the sauce ingredients and cook over a low heat until they thicken, stirring all the time. Keep warm.

2. Marinate the fish pieces in the sherry or rice wine and salt for 30 minutes. Then dip each piece in the cornflour before coating in batter.

3. To prepare the batter, mix the flour, baking powder and egg with 4fl oz (110ml) cold water, and beat well.

4. Meanwhile, bring the oil slowly up to smoking point in a wok or deep-fryer. Dip the pieces of fish in the batter, shake to get rid of any excess, carefully lower into the oil and deep-fry a few at a time until golden brown. Keep the pieces warm while you fry the rest.

5. To serve, arrange the fish on a platter. Pour over the sauce, then decorate with an assortment of radish water lilies, carrot and spring onion knots, spring onion tassels and sweet pepper jewels (see opposite).

Decorative Vegetables

✦ To make radish lilies, cut the top off each radish. Then, using a sharp knife but without cutting right through, make 3 deep vertical cuts in the vegetable, forming 6 segments. Soak in cold water until the cuts open out to form lilies.

✦ To make carrot knots, wash and peel each carrot, and cut into very thin slices lengthways. Cut each slice into very fine strips or julienne. Take each strip and gently tie into a loose knot. If the carrot is very fresh and brittle and refuses to comply, put the strips into boiling water for a few seconds to make them more pliable.

✦ To make spring onion knots, cut the long green leaves into strips, then tie into knots.

✦ To make spring onion tassels, cut most of the green part off (use to make knots), leaving the bulb and about 1 inch (2.5cm) of stalk. Using a sharp knife, carefully cut the green leaves into strips almost to the centre. Alternatively, cut both ends (the green leaves and the bulb) into strips almost to the centre. Put the tassels to soak in a bowl of cold water until they open out.

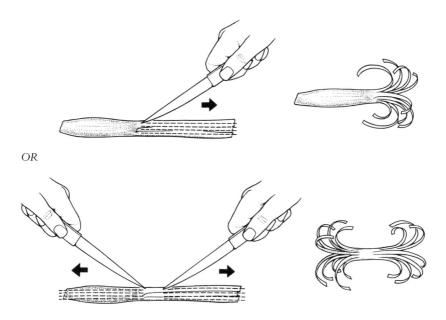

OR

✦ To make pepper jewels, use a selection of green, orange and red peppers. Remove the seeds and most of the pith. Then cut the flesh into diamond jewel shapes and sprinkle over the fish dish. If you have a steady hand (and the time) you could try cutting the pepper into more ornate shapes, like stars and octagons, to resemble other gems.

COCONUT FISH CURRY

❀

THIS IS a Sri Lankan speciality and very good it is! Hot and spicy but with a creamy sweetness due to the coconut milk.

SERVES 4

1 tablespoon chilli powder
1 teaspoon ground turmeric
¼ teaspoon ground cinnamon
3 cloves garlic, peeled and crushed
1 teaspoon grated fresh ginger
1 teaspoon celery salt
1 teaspoon salt
2 onions, peeled and chopped
1lb (450g) fish (e.g. cod, hake, tuna or mackerel), cut into 1 inch (2.5cm) chunks

1 tablespoon oil
1 stalk of lemon grass or the juice and grated rind of 1 lemon
a 2 inch (5cm) piece of *rampe* or pandanus (optional)
5 curry leaves (optional)
3oz (75g) block coconut cream, dissolved in 9fl oz (250ml) hot water

1. Mix the chilli powder, turmeric, cinnamon, garlic and ginger, celery salt, salt and onions in a large bowl. Rub the fish with this and keep to one side for 15 minutes to let the flavours penetrate.

2. Heat the oil in a saucepan and fry the lemon grass (or lemon rind), and *rampe* and curry leaves if using, for a few seconds. Take the fish out of the bowl and add it to the pan. Fry until golden brown, taking care not to let the pieces break up.

3. Lastly, add the mixture in the bowl to the pan, along with the coconut milk. Simmer until the curry is cooked. Stir in the lemon juice if using, and serve.

DEEP-FRIED SPRATS WITH SPICY DIPPING SAUCE

IN SRI LANKA and Malaysia we used to be enthralled by all the little fish which darted in and out of the rock formations in their thousands, like brilliantly coloured, billowing clouds. We confess that we ate neon and angel fish, gold and black guppies and other aquarium favourites without any qualms – they were caught in the fishermen's nets in such profusion.

An East London speciality is crispy fried whitebait or sprats, served with lots of fresh bread and butter and slices of lemon. Try our Oriental version for a change.

SERVES 4

3 tablespoons soy sauce

2 tablespoons sherry

1 teaspoon finely grated fresh ginger

1lb (450g) small fish, e.g. whitebait, sprats or sardines (or empty the aquarium if you have tired of them – only joking!)

2 teaspoons salt

½ teaspoon chilli powder

2 tablespoons cornflour

1 pint (570ml) oil, for deep-frying

1. Prepare the sauce by mixing the soy sauce, sherry and ginger in a saucepan. Bring it to the boil, then allow it to get cold.

2. If the fish are very small there is no need to take off their heads or gut them. Those who are more squeamish can do both. Wash them and dry thoroughly on paper towels.

3. Sprinkle with the salt and chilli powder and leave for 30 minutes.

4. Put the cornflour in a paper or plastic bag. Then put in a few fish at a time and gently shake them until they are lightly covered. Place on a plate and repeat until all the fish are coated.

5. Bring the oil to smoking point in a wok or deep-fryer, and fry the fish in batches until they are crisp and brown.

6. Serve with the dipping sauce, *Sambol Ulek* (p. 28) and thin slices of lime.

SRI LANKAN FISH BALLS

JULIAN, Rani's youngest son, is a money dealer in the City of London, like his brother. We named him 'fruit bat' when he was young because he would gorge on mountains of fruit – his best and most repellent party trick was to eat a banana whole (which he could get in his mouth sideways!).

Recently, to win a £20 bet with another broker, he ate an 8oz (225g) baby octopus (thankfully cooked!) in one mouthful, munching the tentacles which dangled out of the side of his mouth, to the amused horror of his colleagues. He is learning how to cook and is becoming a dab hand at stir-fries and French food especially. This recipe comes highly recommended by him.

SERVES 4

1 × 1lb (450g) tin salmon or tuna, drained
1 small onion, peeled and finely chopped
2 small green chillies, chopped
1 teaspoon salt
½ teaspoon ground black pepper
1 teaspoon each ground coriander and
   cumin
1 large potato, weighing about 8oz (225g),
   peeled, boiled and mashed

1 clove garlic, peeled and crushed
1 teaspoon finely crushed ginger
1 teaspoon lime juice
2 eggs
3 tablespoons flour
1lb (450g) fresh breadcrumbs
1 pint (570ml) oil, for deep-frying

1. Mix all the ingredients, except one egg and the flour, breadcrumbs and oil, in a bowl. Roll into small balls about the size of a large marble or walnut.

2. Break the other egg into a bowl and whisk lightly with a fork. Put the flour and breadcrumbs into two separate bowls. Line them up on a work surface in this order – flour, egg, breadcrumbs, then a large empty plate. You are about to start a production line!

3. Roll the fish balls in the flour, then the egg, then the breadcrumbs, and put them on the plate. Use up all the fish mixture this way.

4. Heat the oil to smoking point in a deep-fryer or wok and fry the balls until golden brown, not too many at a time. This will ensure that the oil stays hot and the balls remain crispy. Garnish with parsley or coriander leaves on a bed of shredded lettuce and serve with Tamarind & Date Dip (p. 43) and *Sambol Ulek* (p. 28).

CHEENA PATAS PRAWNS
CHINESE FIRECRACKER PRAWNS

OUR MOTHER was a Chinese film star, known as a beauty in her day. In fact, she was once walking in London's Soho with my father when she was accosted by a grey-haired old man outside a cinema club (no, not one of those, but one that shows Chinese films exclusively). He had recognised our mother – not bad as she had left the film world in her early thirties and at the time of the encounter she was a mere 81!

When we lived in Sri Lanka, she was plagued by gangs of little boys who would pull the corners of their eyes up with their fingers and shout 'Cheena nona' ('Chinese lady'). This enraged both her and our driver, who needed little encouragement to leg it after them, scattering oaths and backhand swipes. It was all good fun and the boys would run away laughing hysterically, while Mother shook her umbrella at them.

This recipe always reminds us of Mum – a firecracker if ever there was one. *Patas* means 'bang!' in Malay and the frying prawns do sound a bit like crackers going off.

SERVES 4–6

2 large onions, peeled and finely chopped
2 cloves garlic, peeled and finely chopped
2 tablespoons oil
2 teaspoons salt
2lb (1kg) prawns in their shells (uncooked ones are really the best)

1 teaspoon chilli powder
3 tablespoons tomato ketchup
1 tablespoon lemon juice

1. Fry the onions and garlic in the oil until they begin to colour.

2. Add the salt and prawns and stir.

3. Add the rest of the ingredients and fry until they are well blended and the oil begins to separate around the edge of the pan.

4. Serve on a bed of fluffy white rice.

SOUR PRAWN CURRY WITH TAMARIND

A N EASY-TO-MAKE Thai speciality – juicy whole prawns in a clear, hot and spicy sauce.

SERVES 4–6

1lb (450g) raw prawns
1 tablespoon diced fresh garlic
1 tablespoon chopped spring onions
1 teaspoon *blachan* (shrimp paste)

3 tablespoons fish sauce
2oz (50g) tamarind, mixed with 3
  tablespoons hot water and sieved
2 fresh red chillies, chopped

1. Clean the prawns. Take off the heads and shells and remove and discard the dark line running down the back of each one.

2. Put the heads and shells into a pan with 1¼ pints (750ml) water and boil for 10 minutes. Strain and keep the liquid.

3. Pound the garlic and spring onions to a paste, or use an electric blender.

4. Add the rest of the ingredients, except the chillies, to the prawn stock and simmer gently for 5 minutes until the prawns are cooked. Do not overcook or they will toughen and lose their succulence.

5. Stir in the chopped chillies and serve.

SRI LANKAN PRAWN CURRY

IN SRI LANKA we have an amazing range of prawns and shrimps, from tiny, threadlike ones to huge monsters, some 1lb (450g) in weight. Negombo Lagoon tiger prawns are highly prized for their sweetness and succulence. Their name comes from the dark tiger-like stripes on their shells. For this recipe, you need to buy the biggest, best-quality prawns you can find.

SERVES 4–6

1 large onion, peeled and chopped

1 clove garlic, peeled and crushed

2 tablespoons oil

1 teaspoon crushed maldive fish or dried shrimp (optional)

1lb (450g) prawns (raw or the best-quality frozen)

¼ quantity Sri Lankan Curry Sauce (p. 25)

2 medium-sized potatoes, peeled and cut into very small cubes

2 kaffir lime leaves (optional)

1. Fry the onion and garlic in the oil until they begin to turn brown.

2. Add the maldive fish or dried shrimp, if using, and stir for a few seconds more.

3. Lastly add the prawns, curry sauce, 11fl oz (300ml) water, potatoes, and lime leaves if using. Bring to the boil, then reduce the heat and simmer for 10–15 minutes or until the potatoes are cooked.

VARIATIONS

✦ If you prefer a creamier curry, add a 2 inch (5cm) block of coconut cream at the end of the cooking time.

✦ If a sweeter curry is more to your taste, stir in 1 teaspoon paprika, 1 tablespoon tomato purée and 2 chopped tomatoes with the potato at step 3.

LOBSTER CANTONESE

A CLASSIC recipe which is easier to make now that frozen lobsters are so widely available. Nothing beats the taste of a freshly boiled lobster though, so if you are lucky enough to be given the choice always go for a fresh one.

SERVES 4–6

2 × 1lb (450g) lobsters
1 tablespoon soy sauce
1 teaspoon sherry
1 teaspoon sugar
½ teaspoon salt
4fl oz (110ml) Homemade Chicken Stock
   (p. 33) or ½ chicken stock cube dissolved
   in the same quantity of boiling water
3 tablespoons oil

1 teaspoon crushed ginger
2 cloves garlic, peeled and crushed
2 tablespoons black beans, soaked in water
   then crushed (optional)
4oz (110g) minced pork
2 tablespoons cornflour, mixed with
   2 tablespoons water
2 very fresh free-range eggs, beaten

1. Clean the lobsters, throwing away the stomach and gills. Chop each into 2 inch (5cm) pieces with a cleaver.

2. Mix the soy sauce, sherry, sugar, salt and stock and keep to one side.

3. Heat the oil in a wok. When hot, fry the ginger and garlic for 30 seconds, then the black beans if using, and pork, and fry for a further 2–3 minutes or until the pork is no longer pink.

4. Add the lobster, heat through, then remove to a warmed dish.

5. Add the stock and cornflour paste to the wok and stir until thick. Add the lobster and heat through.

6. Take the wok off the heat and add the raw eggs in a thin stream, stirring until they set in thin threads. If there is not enough heat, return to a gentle heat until they do. Do not overcook.

STUFFED SQUID

A LOT OF people avoided squid in the past because they could not be bothered to clean and prepare them. But these days cleaned and frozen squid hoods are frequently available. Squid makes lovely eating as long as it is cooked correctly. If not, you will find chewing on a rubber boot infinitely more satisfying! Choose small squid, as they will be the youngest and most tender.

In South-East Asian and Oriental kitchens, squid is cooked for no more than a minute or two – just long enough to turn the flesh opaque. Stir-frying is ideal. Alternatively, the hoods make excellent containers for a number of special stuffings. The opening is sewn up with needle and thread or secured with cocktail sticks and the squid is steamed. When cooked it is sliced into rings and served on a dish – very spectacular.

SERVES 4–6

8oz (225g) minced pork

4 tablespoons chopped drained water chestnuts

1 spring onion, washed, trimmed and finely chopped

2 tablespoons hoi sin sauce

1 clove garlic, peeled and crushed

1 teaspoon *tung choi* (preserved Chinese vegetable), chopped (optional)

½ teaspoon sesame oil (optional)

1 egg

1 teaspoon salt

½ teaspoon ground white pepper

1 teaspoon cornflour

4 squid hoods, weighing about 1lb (450g), cleaned and dried

1. Mix all the ingredients together in a large bowl and loosely stuff the squid hoods. Don't pack them with too much stuffing or they may burst while cooking.

2. Sew the openings up with a needle and thread or use cocktail sticks to close.

3. Lay the squid in a single layer, and steam them over boiling water for 15 minutes or until they feel tender when prodded with a fork.

4. Remove the threads or cocktail sticks and cut the squid into slices. Lay on a bed of Fried 'Seaweed' (p. 51) and serve with dipping sauces such as Tiger Lily's Special Sweet & Sour Sauce (p. 30), Vietnamese Fish Sauce (p. 29) or *Nam Prik* (p. 27).

5. Any leftover stuffing should be rolled into small balls (use some cornflour if it feels too sticky), then gently fried in a little oil and served with the squid and dipping sauces.

STIR-FRIED SQUID WITH VEGETABLES

THIS IS a dish which we predict will quickly become a favourite. The squid is blanched in hot oil for a few seconds only, then stir-fried with the vegetables, to ensure that it remains tender.

SERVES 6

2lb (900g) squid, cleaned, dried and fancy-cut into 1½ inch (4cm) squares

2 tablespoons sherry

2 teaspoons cornflour

1 teaspoon freshly grated ginger

1 pint (570ml) oil, for deep-frying

4 dried Chinese mushrooms, sliced and soaked

4 spring onions, washed, trimmed and chopped

4oz (110g) mange tout, each cut diagonally into 3

2 teaspoons salt

1 teaspoon sugar

½ teaspoon *Sambol Ulek* (p. 28), or ½ teaspoon black beans, mashed

½ teaspoon sesame oil

1. Put the squid in a bowl with 1 tablespoon of the sherry, the cornflour and ginger, and leave to marinate for 20 minutes.

2. Heat the cooking oil in a wok, then fry the squid for 30 seconds only in small batches. Be prepared to work quickly – the squid only needs to turn white before being whisked out and dried on paper towels. Keep warm.

3. Carefully pour out all but 2 tablespoons of oil from the wok. Return the wok to the stove and heat until it begins to smoke.

4. Stir-fry the mushrooms and spring onions for 1½ minutes.

5. Add the mange tout, salt, sugar, remaining sherry and *sambol ulek* or black beans. Stir for 1 minute.

6. Finally, add the squid and sesame oil, stir and serve.

VARIATION

✦ This is a very pretty dish with the white squid contrasting with the black mushrooms and green spring onions. If you wish, you can make it look even prettier by sprinkling a pinch of sesame seeds over the top before serving.

Decorative Squid

✦ Squid can be cut in different ways when raw to look decorative. Remember not to slice completely through the skin – only score the top surface about halfway through.

Cut the hood vertically, open it out like a book and lay it flat, inner side down. When you have marked out the patterns (see below), cut the squid into squares ready for cooking.

✦ For a diamond cut, use a very sharp vegetable knife and carefully score the skin into diamonds by making long diagonal cuts first in one direction, then the other.

✦ For a porcupine cut, use a pair of kitchen scissors to make random V-shaped snips over the whole surface, all facing the same direction. Very young squid with thin skins are not suitable, as you are likely to cut right through.

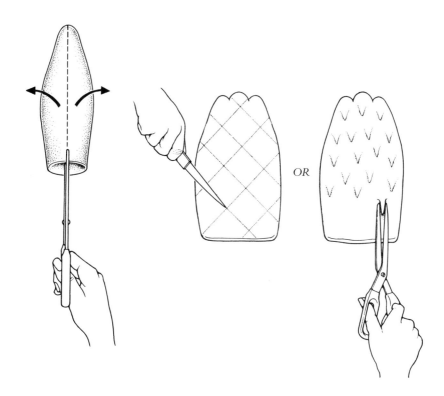

OR

CRAB CURRY

JUST THE words make us drool! Our parents had friends in Sri Lanka called the De Jongs who owned a pig farm. We, and an odd assortment of friends we knew from embassies abroad, had very memorable parties at their house. A large pig would be spit-roasted over an open pit and the outside tables would be groaning with dishes of curries, rice, stringhoppers, salads and breads. We would dance under a velvety black sky, in the light of a huge tropical moon, with lemon-scented flares to keep the mosquitoes at bay.

To drink, we were given fresh iced lime or passion fruit juice, or Portello (a dark mixed fruit fizzy drink). The men, especially, downed bottles of *arrack* – a smooth coconut liquor not unlike whisky, packing a dangerous punch!

After eating the pig and nearly everything else, at about 1am, just when we were beginning to wilt, out would come the highlight of the evening – steaming cauldrons of soft-shelled Negombo Lagoon crab curry to eat with *rotis*. Nothing could have tasted as wonderful then or since. This recipe evokes those very happy, very gluttonous memories.

SERVES 6

4–5 crabs, weighing approximately
  3lb (1.4kg)
1–2 teaspoons chilli powder
2 teaspoons ground coriander
2 teaspoons Roasted Sri Lankan Curry
  Powder (p. 20)
a 2 inch (5cm) piece of cinnamon, crushed
2 large onions, peeled, chopped and
  liquidised with 1½–2 pints (425ml–1.2
  litres) water
3 teaspoons salt
½ teaspoon dill seeds

2 tablespoons coconut or vegetable oil
6 curry leaves (optional)
1 stalk lemon grass, chopped
a 2 inch (5cm) piece of *rampe* or pandanus
  (optional)
6 onions, peeled and sliced
1 teaspoon malt vinegar
2 teaspoons ground turmeric
2 limes, de-seeded and cut into pieces
3½ oz (100g) block coconut cream, cut into
  small cubes

1. Clean each crab, discarding the stomach and gills. Remove the big claws and bash them gently with the back of a knife so the sauce can permeate the meat. Don't be too enthusiastic or you will be picking pieces of shell out of the finished dish! Take off the smaller claws, and reserve. Chop the body into 4 pieces.

2. Dry-roast the chilli, coriander, curry powder and crushed cinnamon in a pan for a few minutes, taking care not to burn the mixture. When it begins to darken, add all the remaining ingredients, except the coconut cream, bring to the boil then gently simmer for 20 minutes.

3. Stir the coconut cream in gently, just before serving. Do not boil, as the curry may curdle.

VARIATIONS

✦ Two ingredients which we have not been able to track down in the West are goraka and murunga leaves. Goraka is an orange fruit which turns black when dried in the sun. It is very sour and adds a deep sharp flavour to this and other savoury dishes. If you can get it, omit the limes and add 2 pieces goraka, weighing about 4oz (110g), instead.

✦ Murunga trees are very slim and beautiful. Their feathery leaves resemble mimosa leaves and their fruits are long 'drumsticks' which we make into curry. These can be bought in speciality shops. We make murunga leaves into sambols, too. For this recipe we would add 2 large sprigs of leaves, finely chopped. There is no substitute.

ABALONE OR SCALLOPS WITH CHICKEN & ASPARAGUS

A DELICIOUS dish, combining the sweetness and melting tenderness of the clam with asparagus, the king of vegetables. Scallops, too, are delicious cooked this way. The shortest possible cooking time is needed for these prized shellfish – only until the flesh turns opaque – and don't even think of reheating them.

SERVES 6–8

1 × 15oz (425g) tin abalone, drained and rinsed in water *or* 1lb (450g) frozen scallops, defrosted

1 × 15oz (425g) tin asparagus spears, drained, *or* fresh spears, lightly steamed, refreshed in cold water, then drained immediately

1 teaspoon salt

3 teaspoons cornflour

8oz (225g) chicken breast, finely sliced

1 tablespoon melted chicken fat or oil

1 tablespoon sweet sherry or ginger wine

½ teaspoon sugar

10fl oz (275ml) Homemade Chicken Stock (p. 33) or ½ chicken stock cube dissolved in the same quantity of water

1. Cut the abalone into thin slices or the scallops into chunks. Each should be a mouthful in size.

2. Reserve half the asparagus for garnish and chop the rest into 2 inch (5cm) pieces.

3. Mix ½ teaspoon salt and 1 teaspoon cornflour together and use to coat the chicken.

4. Heat the fat or oil in a wok. When smoking, stir-fry the chicken for a few seconds. Add the fish, stir-fry for a few seconds more, then add the asparagus pieces, sherry, sugar, the remaining salt and the stock.

5. Mix the remaining cornflour with 4 tablespoons water to form a cream. Add to the wok and bring to the boil. Stir until the sauce thickens, then place on a serving dish, decorate with the reserved asparagus tips and serve.

OPPOSITE *Clockwise from top:* Simple Malay Chicken Satay (page 95), served with Satay Sauce (page 32), Fried Rice Sticks with Seafood and Vegetables (page 90), Sri Lankan Hoppers (page 74), Pao (page 78), Stuffed Spring Rolls (page 50)

Vegetables

WE ARE very fortunate to have experienced life in the East. We were both born in Bangkok and then moved to Sri Lanka. Sudden violent tropical storms, followed by intense sunshine, would make the earth hiss and steam, encouraging miraculously lush vegetation.

Everything seemed to grow with very little assistance – rubbish dumps would be smothered with tomato, cucumber, melon, pawpaw and other plants. A papaya (or pawpaw) seed planted at the beginning of the year would bear its first luscious fruit within six months and continue to bear fruit more than once a year! Planting a single stalk of lemon grass would result in a small forest within a surprisingly short time.

Chopping down a banana plant, once its comb of bananas was harvested, would encourage new plants to spring up around the original site (bananas grow from rhizomes and can pop up anywhere along the rhizome's length). Even bare sticks pushed into the ground for picket fences would sprout and flower.

Market day was always a treat for us. Grinning toothless old ladies, their gums stained orange by chewing betel (a tobacco-like plant), would walk many miles with huge flat wicker baskets on their heads, bearing a profusion of vegetables and fruit which could be bought for a few rupees. We loved their fat shiny purple aubergines, the long snake beans and gourds, the red Bombay onions, the chillies of all colours and sizes (the smallest being the deadliest!) and other home-grown produce.

In this book we have tried to select more unusual vegetable (and fruit) recipes for you to try. They are easy to follow – and, as always, you can substitute other vegetables if you wish. You may be enchanted (as we were) to learn that there is one Sri Lankan recipe which involves dipping hibiscus flowers in batter and deep-frying them.

OPPOSITE *Clockwise from top:* Indonesian Grilled Spicy Chicken (page 113), Stir-Fried Beans (page 146), Coconut Rotis (page 76)

MALLUNG
DRY GREENS & SPICY COCONUT VEGETABLES

❧

THIS IS the Asian equivalent of stir-frying and a way of cooking green vegetable leaves so that all the nutrients are preserved. Use cabbage, cauliflower (both the white 'head' and tender leaves surrounding it), spinach or spring greens, or a mixture of all of them. First soak the leaves in salted water to get rid of any insects, rinse thoroughly, then shred very finely with a sharp knife.

Although this is a spicy dish, the flavours are not overpowering so it would sit quite happily on the table with Western foods.

Leftover *mallung*, when mixed with an equal amount of mashed potato and fried in a little oil like a large pancake, takes good old British 'bubble and squeak' into another dimension.

SERVES 4

1lb (450g) shredded greens
½ teaspoon ground turmeric
2 teaspoons ground maldive fish or dried
    prawns (optional)
2 teaspoons lime or lemon juice

1 teaspoon salt
1 teaspoon chilli powder
½ teaspoon sugar
3 tablespoons desiccated coconut

1. Put all the ingredients, except the coconut, into a heavy-based frying pan and stir over a moderate heat for 3–4 minutes. If the leaves start turning brown, add a tiny amount of water (no more than 2 tablespoons).

2. Add the coconut and stir until the mixture is dry.

3. Serve lukewarm, as a side dish, with rice and curries.

CHANNA

SPICY CHICKPEAS

THIS IS a firm favourite with Chandra's family – she always serves it at family gatherings and none of us has tired of it yet! A deliciously nutty and lightly fragrant dish, it is good with rice or *rotis*. In Sri Lanka it is the equivalent of chips – served in paper cones on every street corner. Johnnie, Chandra's youngest, is a lover of fast foods, to our disapproval. However Channa is also one of his very favourite things – he eats it by the bucketful!

SERVES 4–6

2 × 14oz (400g) tins chickpeas, *or* 12oz
   (350g) dry chickpeas, soaked overnight
   in 4 pints (2 litres) water
3 tablespoons oil
1 large onion, peeled and chopped
1 teaspoon salt
1 teaspoon ground black pepper

2 teaspoons ground cumin
1 teaspoon chilli powder
½ teaspoon ground turmeric
½ teaspoon ground coriander
¼ teaspoon garlic powder
2 tablespoons lemon juice
some chopped coriander leaves

1. Drain the tinned chickpeas. Or, if using dried chickpeas, rinse them, cover with water, then simmer for 45 minutes or until tender.

2. Heat the oil in a pan and fry the onion until soft and turning brown.

3. Add the rest of the ingredients (except for the fresh coriander) and stir for about 3 minutes over a medium heat. Take care not to burn – add a little water if necessary.

4. Turn into a bowl, garnish with the chopped coriander, and serve.

VARIATION

✦ Garnish with rings of fresh, thinly sliced onion and tomato; or sprinkle with ground dried maldive fish or prawns.

DRY POTATO & COCONUT CURRY

W E KNOW we keep saying this is the easiest recipe ever but do try this one – it must at least be a runner up for the title!

SERVES 4

2 large potatoes, weighing approximately 1lb (450g), washed and dried	1 tablespoon oil 4oz (110g) Coconut Sambol (p. 34)

1. Prick the potatoes and either put in a microwave on full power for 3 minutes each or boil in their skins until half-cooked. Do not peel but cut into chunks about 1 inch (2.5cm) in size.

2. Heat the oil in a pan, add the potatoes and fry until just beginning to brown – 3–5 minutes.

3. Add the coconut sambol, stir for 1 minute more, and serve.

VARIATION

✦ If a more substantial dish is wanted, add 8oz (225g) cooked peeled prawns and a diced green pepper to the potatoes at step 2.

OKRA CURRY

ALTHOUGH our tastes in food are similar (we tend to eat anything!) the family is sharply divided over okra (or ladies fingers). Neither Mum nor Rani can abide its gooey flesh and seeds, while Chandra and Dad simply adore it. As a result, Dad has learnt how to cook this Sri Lankan dish but in half the usual quantity.

Okra curry can be made the day before but it does not take kindly to being frozen.

SERVES 4

8oz (225g) okra or ladies fingers, washed and dried

4 tablespoons oil

½ teaspoon ground turmeric

2 teaspoons salt

1 teaspoon each ground cumin and coriander

1 tablespoon ground maldive fish or dried prawns

3 green chillies, chopped

3 small onions, peeled and chopped

1 teaspoon chilli powder

4 curry leaves (optional)

a 2 inch (5cm) piece *rampe* (pandanus, optional)

1oz (25g) block coconut cream, mixed with 11fl oz (300ml) hot water

1. Top and tail the okra. If large, cut each into 3 parts; if smaller, cut into 2.

2. Heat the oil in a saucepan, add the okra, turmeric and salt and stir-fry for about 4 minutes or until the okra turns a light golden brown. Remove with a slotted spoon and put on one side.

3. Add all the remaining ingredients, except the coconut milk, to the same oil and fry until brown over a medium heat. Take care that it doesn't burn.

4. Return the fried okra to the pan, add the coconut milk and simmer gently for about 8 minutes or until a little oil begins to appear on the top of the dish.

5. Serve hot.

GADO GADO

INDONESIAN SALAD

WITH THIS dish you can really express your artistic soul! Why not decorate with flowers instead of the eggs? The different colours of the ingredients are quite stunning. If you choose to use several smaller plates, they can take the place of traditional floral arrangements on your buffet table. Just take care not to overcook the different vegetables. You may wish to place a small card on the table in front of this dish to explain that the sauce contains peanuts, for anyone who may suffer from an allergic reaction to them.

If making this for a party, it's best to prepare the vegetables the day before and keep them overnight, covered with foil or clingfilm, in the refrigerator. Quarter the eggs just before serving.

We do not pour the satay sauce over the whole platter, but serve it in bowls alongside. This allows your guests to make their choice of seasoning. Served with a selection of cooked prawns, chicken breast, sliced meats, *Nam Prik* (p. 27), *Sambol Ulek* (p. 28) and various chilli sauces, this colourful salad will form the main focus of a buffet table.

SERVES 6–8

½ small white cabbage

8oz (225g) French or bobby beans

4oz (110g) carrots

2 medium-sized potatoes

4oz (110g) bean sprouts

¼ small cucumber, finely sliced or cut into batons

8oz (225g) tomatoes, cut into quarters

3 hard-boiled eggs, shelled and quartered, or a selection of edible flowers

1 quantity Satay Sauce (p. 32)

2 spring onions, washed, trimmed and chopped

1. Shred the cabbage, and top and tail the beans and break them into 1 inch (2.5cm) lengths. Scrape the carrots and cut into sticks similar in size to the beans.

2. Wash the potatoes, cut them into wedges, and boil in their skins for about 4 minutes, or until just cooked.

3. Steam the cabbage, beans, bean sprouts and carrots separately until each is just cooked, then immediately refresh by putting them in a colander and running cold water over them. The carrots should take no more than 3 minutes, the beans 2 minutes and the bean sprouts and cabbage only 1 minute. This brief cooking helps retain all the colour and flavour. Place the vegetables on a large plate.

4. Add the cucumber to the plate with the quartered tomatoes and eggs, if using, or the flowers.

5. Make up the satay sauce and serve in small bowls, or pour on top of the vegetable platter and sprinkle the chopped spring onions over the top.

Pineapple curry

PINEAPPLES grow like weeds in Sri Lanka and many swear by their apparent slimming properties. Rani once lost nearly 2 stone (10kg) in just over eight weeks by eating pineapples every day. Then again, it might have been because the temperature in Sri Lanka at the time was in the high 80s and very humid too.

SERVES 3–4

1 medium-sized fresh pineapple or 2 × 1lb (450g) tins pineapple chunks, drained
1 dessertspoon ground maldive fish or dried prawns
½ teaspoon each chilli powder, ground cinnamon and cumin
1 teaspoon ground turmeric
1 teaspoon salt
1 dessertspoon oil
1 teaspoon whole mustard seeds
1 dessertspoon sliced onions
2 green chillies, chopped
grated rind of 1 lemon
4oz (110g) block coconut cream, mixed with 4fl oz (110ml) hot water

1. Remove the skin and 'eyes' from the fresh pineapple. Dice the pineapple and mix with all the dry ingredients except the mustard seeds.

2. Heat the oil in a saucepan, add the mustard seeds and stir until they 'pop'.

3. Add the onions and fry until they begin to brown.

4. Put all the remaining ingredients in the saucepan and simmer gently for 10–15 minutes, adding a little extra water if the curry gets too dry. Do not bring to the boil or the coconut milk will curdle.

VARIATION
◆ Add a few curry leaves, a 1 inch (2.5cm) piece *rampe* (pandanus) and a little lemon grass to the curry as it simmers.

CASHEW NUT CURRY

A DELIGHTFUL dish which is full of protein and deliciously 'meaty'. This recipe is a great favourite with vegetarians and we confess that we do not need meat when this is the main dish. In cashew season in Sri Lanka, the very prettiest girls are seen with great baskets of the nuts by the roadside on the way to Kandy where the University of Peredeniya is situated.

When the Queen visited the University she said it was one of the most beautiful she had ever seen. It is built of pink stone and is surrounded by flowering trees which rain down a constant shower of pink petals. Our dad's only brother, Professor Gerald Cooray, is a world-famous geologist and lives in Kandy with his wife Joan. For many years he taught at Peredeniya.

The cashew hangs like a pearl from the end of a large fruit, from which an interesting jam and curry is made. As neither the cashew sellers nor their fruit are seen in the West, we will share this recipe with you instead.

SERVES 3–4

8oz (225g) raw unsalted cashew nuts

1 tablespoon oil

1 medium onion, peeled and finely chopped

1½ teaspoons ground coriander

1 teaspoon ground cumin

¼ teaspoon ground turmeric

2 cloves

3 cardamom pods, crushed

1 stick of cinnamon

1 teaspoon salt

2oz (50g) block coconut cream, mixed with 11fl oz (300ml) hot water

1 small green chilli, chopped

4 curry leaves (optional)

1. Soak the cashew nuts in water overnight. The next day, rinse and dry the nuts on paper towels.

2. Heat the oil in a pan and fry the onion until soft and beginning to turn brown.

3. Add the rest of the ingredients, bring to the boil, then lower the heat and simmer for 15 minutes.

MIXED VEGETABLE STIR-FRY

EVERYONE has a special vegetable stir-fry recipe. This is one of our favourites because of the contrasts in colour and texture. But feel free to add your own ingredients – and never be afraid to experiment.

When we first started selling our products at car boot sales, and then at trade fairs, we lost count of the number of enquiries from people who were afraid of experimenting. If we suggested spreading a teaspoon of one of our relishes over a lamb chop and then grilling it, we were invariably asked if it would be 'all right' to put it on a pork chop or even a chicken joint. We would say 'Put it on your old man's socks if you think he'll eat it!'. Many think that Oriental and South-East Asian cooking is more difficult than it really is.

Nothing gives us greater delight nowadays than meeting those early 'is-it-all-right-to-put-it-on-a-pork-chop?' customers who have kept in touch, become friends and now tell us of amazing new ways to use our products.

SERVES 4–6

4oz (110g) *pak choi* (Chinese cabbage) or spinach

2oz (50g) each whole baby sweetcorn, broccoli florets, mange tout, button mushrooms, canned water chestnuts and bamboo shoots

2 teaspoons vegetable oil

1 clove garlic, peeled and crushed

1 thin slice of ginger, crushed

1 tablespoon soy sauce

1 teaspoon salt

½ teaspoon sugar

1 teaspoon cornflour, mixed with 1 tablespoon sherry

1 teaspoon sesame oil (optional)

1. Wash all the vegetables. Cut the cabbage or spinach into strips. Leave the sweetcorn whole if it is very small (about the size of a baby's finger) or cut into 2 if any bigger. Break the broccoli into small florets, and cut the mushrooms and water chestnuts in half. Slice the bamboo shoots into strips.

2. Put the cabbage, sweetcorn, broccoli and mange tout into a pan of boiling water, cook for no more than 1 minute, then strain in a colander and place under cold running water to refresh.

3. Heat a large wok, add the vegetable oil and, when hot, add the garlic and ginger and swirl them around. Add all the vegetables and stir-fry for 2 minutes only.

4. Add the soy sauce, salt and sugar, and the cornflour and sherry mixture. Stir to thicken, add the sesame oil, and serve immediately.

STIR-FRIED BEANS

Tᴴɪꜱ ɪꜱ another of our favourite vegetable recipes. Use either French beans or runner beans. Just ensure that they are at their youngest and snappiest best. No stringy old has-beans (excuse the pun!) for this dish please.

SERVES 4–6

1 tablespoon oil

1 clove garlic, peeled and crushed

1 thin slice of ginger, shredded

2oz (50g) unsmoked streaky bacon, cut into small strips

1lb (450g) fresh garden beans, washed, topped and tailed and cut into short lengths

1 tablespoon soy sauce

1 teaspoon sugar

1 teaspoon salt

1. Heat a wok, add the oil and swirl it around. Put the garlic, ginger and bacon in the wok and stir-fry for 1 minute.

2. Add the beans, and the remaining ingredients, with 1 teaspoon water, and stir-fry for a further 3 minutes.

VARIATIONS

✦ Vegetarians can leave out the bacon.

✦ Add a splash of fish sauce and a small chopped chilli at the end, to give this dish a more Thai flavour.

STIR-FRIED CHINESE CABBAGE WITH PRAWNS OR SHRIMPS

ONLY A FEW years ago the great British public were very wary of 'foreign things' like garlic and ginger. Now a plethora of ingredients can be bought everywhere, from supermarkets to corner shops. Our greatest delight is to go to Chinatown in London and see the huge lorries from local farms unload their harvest which includes nearly every conceivable Chinese and Oriental vegetable, from different green leaves to winter melon and long 'snake' beans. Wonderful!

However we had to make do with ordinary white cabbage for so long that we now enjoy either version of this dish.

1 small white cabbage or *pak choi*, weighing approximately 1lb (450g)

2 tablespoons oil

2 spring onions, washed, trimmed and chopped

2 tablespoons soy sauce

1 teaspoon sugar

1 teaspoon ginger wine or sweet sherry (optional)

1 teaspoon cornflour, mixed with 1 tablespoon water

2oz (50g) cooked peeled prawns or shrimps

salt and pepper (optional)

1. Wash the cabbage or *pak choi*, then shred finely with a sharp knife.

2. Heat a wok and add the oil. When smoking, add the cabbage and stir-fry for 3 minutes.

3. Add the rest of the ingredients and stir-fry until the prawns or shrimps are warmed through and the sauce thickens. Taste and add extra salt and pepper if necessary.

VARIATIONS

✦ Vegetarians can omit the prawns, and substitute 2oz (50g) sliced mushrooms instead.

✦ If you wish, sprinkle a little ground dried prawns over this dish when serving, to further deepen the taste of the fresh prawns.

Bean sprouts

Bean sprouts are everyone's favourite, especially our mother's. She goes wild for the larger, firmer soya bean sprouts which are available from Chinese speciality stores. Sprouts are very nutritious and raw bean sprouts are delicious added to green salads, giving a satisfying crunch to every mouthful. Although bean sprouts are available from most supermarkets, they are very easy to grow. Try harvesting your own soya bean or mung bean (the smaller, more familiar) sprouts. Seeds are readily available from wholefood shops. Just tell the shopkeeper you want to sprout them and gather the following items:

2 tablespoons or 2oz (50g) mung or soya beans

1 large glass jar

a small piece of cheesecloth or thick J-cloth to cover the mouth of the jar

1 large rubber band to go round the neck of the jar

1. Wash the beans thoroughly in plenty of clean water. Put them into the jar and secure the cloth with a rubber band around the rim.

2. Place the jar on its side on a tray and put in a dark warm place – an airing cupboard is ideal.

3. Take the jar out twice a day and rinse with water. The seeds should be fully sprouted within four days or so. Do not let them grow green leaves, as these make the sprouts bitter.

4. Wash very well in fresh water, then top and tail them ready for use.

QUICK FRIED BEAN SPROUTS

SERVES 4–6

1 tablespoon oil

3 spring onions, washed, trimmed and chopped

1lb (450g) bean sprouts

1½ teaspoons cornflour

3 tablespoons Homemade Chicken Stock (p. 33) or use ⅛ chicken stock cube dissolved in 2 tablespoons boiling water

½ teaspoon salt

½ teaspoon garlic salt

a pinch of sugar

1. Heat a wok and add the oil. When it begins to smoke, throw in the spring onions and stir-fry for 30 seconds.

2. Add the bean sprouts and fry until they become translucent.

3. Mix the cornflour with the stock and add to the pan, together with the salt, garlic salt and sugar.

4. Heat through for a further minute, and serve.

VARIATION

✦ As always, you can add what you like to this recipe – any sliced meats, and extra vegetables like shredded cabbage, grated carrot, mushrooms or bamboo shoots. Just remember that bean sprouts are mainly water and only need the minimum cooking time. Cook whatever ingredients you use in sequence, according to how long they need to cook. For instance, meat or fibrous vegetables should be stir-fried after the spring onions but well before the bean sprouts.

Sweets

ORIENTAL and South-East Asian meals do not end traditionally with a 'sweet', as in the West. As we have our choice of delicious fruits, we tend to choose them instead. We used to enjoy sweet treats during the day, or for 'tiffin' at 3pm when everything really did 'stop for tea'. Sri Lankan sweetmeats are quite heavy going – usually stodgy, very sweet and deep-fried in coconut oil. Thula balls, for instance, are made by kneading together jaggery (palm sugar) and sesame seeds until the mixture sticks together and is then formed into balls.

Delicious Muscat (p. 152) is offered to guests who always feel free to pop in. (One thing we at first found strange in the West was the odd practice of waiting to be formally invited.) We also used to enjoy eating curds – very thick, acidic buffalo or cow's milk yoghurt sold in round clay pots by the wayside – mixed with jaggery or freshly harvested honey.

We have included our favourite family recipes in this chapter. Many are inspired by sweets we have tasted in the past but some are treats we invented ourselves to keep our own kids happy when they were small. Those who are young at heart will, we hope, relish them as much.

TURTLE 'EGGS'

RANI TOOK Dad to Singapore and Malaysia in the late eighties. Disorientated from jet lag, Dad slipped in the bathroom on the first night and had to be admitted to hospital for a week with severe concussion. Although very frail, after he was discharged, he insisted we all resume our journey to the east coast to see the gigantic leatherback turtles lay their eggs.

Because of intense tourist interest the turtle numbers had been dwindling, as the reptiles sought quieter beaches to lay their eggs. The manager of our resort warned us not to be disappointed if we did not see any – they tended to come to lay in the early hours of the morning and they went to remote parts of the beach. There was no way we could get Dad, who was still very shaky, to these far-off beaches, and he could not be left on his own.

On the second morning at 9am, in broad daylight, a huge turtle hauled her way out of the water, tears streaming down her face, and laid a clutch of eggs directly in front of Dad's beach hut. It was magical and inexplicable and the manager took photographs of all of us with the turtle for visitor postcards.

These sweet rice dumplings look like turtle eggs. They are as smooth and waxy in appearance, though many times smaller of course. They make a refreshing ending to a meal consisting of a number of rich, savoury main dishes.

SERVES 4–6

4oz (110g) glutinous rice powder (get it from a Chinese food supplier – there is no substitute)

1 tablespoon sugar
1 teaspoon almond essence
1 pint (570ml) full-cream milk

1. Mix the rice powder with 1 teaspoon of the sugar and 2 tablespoons water to form a soft but stiff dough. Add more water if the mixture seems too stiff. Break off tiny amounts, about the size of a marble, and roll into rounds.

2. Put the rest of the sugar, almond essence and milk into a pan and bring it almost to the boil. Watch that it doesn't boil over!

3. Drop in the 'eggs' and simmer for about 3 minutes. They will rise to the surface when cooked.

4. Turtle eggs are delicious served hot or chilled. Add a few crushed ice cubes if they are served cold.

MUSCAT

❀

MUSCAT is somewhat similar to very fragrant Turkish delight but we believe it is far superior. Serve it in very small quantities, as it is so rich.

Our paternal grandfather's brother, Johnnie Cooray, was married to a very sweet lady called Jessie. She spoke no English, only Singhalese which we could not understand, but she was very fond of us. We always pestered Mum and Dad to make a detour after church to stop by their house. When we did, Aunty Jessie would give us lots of kisses and cuddles and, of course, mountains of home-made sweets, particularly muscat, as she knew we loved it so much.

We would like to dedicate this recipe to the Sri Lankan cricket team of 1996 who won the World Cup against all the odds. The sheer exuberance and fine effort of this young team, against the sad background of terrorist activity in Sri Lanka, certainly helped give our people something to dance about in the streets! The Sri Lankan flag is a lion proudly holding a sword. The predominant colours are green, yellow and orange, and we like to colour our muscat accordingly (see Variation opposite).

12oz (350g) flour
3lb (1.35kg) white sugar
10fl oz (275ml) full-cream milk
2oz (50g) raw unsalted cashew nuts, cut
  into slivers

seeds from 3 cardamom pods, crushed
4fl oz (110ml) rosewater
8oz (225g) ghee, melted

1. Mix the flour with a little water and form into a ball. Tie in a clean tea towel.

2. Put into a bowl and add 2 pints (1.15 litres) water.

3. Swish the ball in the water and keep moving it until all the starch comes out. Do this at least 4–5 times, until you are left with just a sticky ball of gluten in the tea towel. Discard this residue.

4. Put the starch water and sugar in a heavy-based saucepan. Bring to the boil, reduce the heat and keep stirring.

5. After about 45 minutes the mixture should turn very thick. Add the milk, cashews, crushed cardamom and rosewater, then add the ghee, spoonful by spoonful. When it turns thick and transparent, take off the heat.

6. Spread onto a well-buttered tray, and leave to set at room temperature.

7. Cut into small chunks and eat with bliss!

VARIATION

✦ To replicate the 3 colours of the Sri Lankan flag, omit the rosewater at step 5. When the mixture turns thick and transparent, take off the heat and divide into 3 equal portions. Colour and flavour 1 portion with 1 teaspoon vanilla essence and a few drops of yellow colouring, 1 portion with 1 teaspoon pistachio essence and a few drops of green colouring, and the last portion with 1 teaspoon orange flower water or orange essence and a few drops of orange colouring.

VATTALAPAN

MANY SRI LANKAN desserts are very oily and heavy, made with coconut and rice flour and deep-fried in coconut oil. Heart attack material! Vattalapan is an exception – a dark, deliciously aromatic custard made with coconut milk and palm sugar and flavoured with cardamom and rosewater. Serve in small portions to begin with – rest assured your guests will come back for seconds or even thirds!

SERVES 6–8

5oz (150g) jaggery (palm sugar) or dark brown sugar	½ teaspoon ground cardamom
	½ teaspoon ground mixed spice
1 × 7oz (200g) block coconut cream, mixed with 1 pint (570ml) hot water	3 teaspoons rosewater
	12 raw unsalted cashew nuts, halved
6 eggs (size 3)	

1. Heat the sugar, coconut cream and hot water in a pan to dissolve gently.

2. Beat the rest of the ingredients, except the cashew nuts, together until frothy, then add to the coconut milk mixture.

3. Pour into a 2 pint (900ml) well-buttered container or 6–8 well-buttered individual heatproof dishes and steam until the custard sets.

4. Decorate with the cashew nuts and serve cold.

OPPOSITE page 152 *Clockwise from top:* Pineapple Curry (page 143), Tomato, Cucumber and Onion Sambol (page 36), Channa (page 139), Roti Djala (page 77).

OPPOSITE *Top to bottom:* Avocado Ice Cream (page 160) served on Sharp Fruit Sauce (page 161), Almond Tea (page 154)

ALMOND TEA

ALTHOUGH very simple to prepare, this sweet is so pretty and refreshing to the palate that our recipe has gone around the world many times, having been much requested by friends and family. The small opaque diamonds of almond cream float in crystal-clear, sweetened ice water. It's very pretty served in a hollowed-out water melon or ice bowl (pp. 156–7).

SERVES 4–6

4oz (110g) sugar
2 × 1oz (30g) sachets Davis gelatine

2 large tins evaporated milk
½ teaspoon almond essence

1. Heat 2oz (50g) sugar with 8fl oz (225ml) water to make a syrup. Then cool and refrigerate.

2. Heat the remaining 2oz (50g) sugar and 8fl oz (225ml) water in a pan to dissolve.

3. Sprinkle the gelatine on top and warm in a saucepan until the gelatine dissolves.

4. Mix in the evaporated milk and almond essence, then pour into a large shallow baking tray or two Swiss roll tins (rinsed in water). Refrigerate until set.

5. Cut into diamond shapes, then serve with the ice cold syrup in a pretty glass bowl. Float a few rose petals on top.

STEAMED BUTTER CAKE

O N A QUICK stroll around any of Chinatown's bakeries you will always see a display of large fluffy golden slabs of this cake. Unlike Western cakes, which are baked, this one is steamed which gives it an interesting texture and lightness. Serve it in chunks, with whipped cream flavoured with a little ginger wine and sliced crystallised ginger.

SERVES 4–6

2 large eggs
½ teaspoon salt
4oz (110g) sugar
3oz (75g) butter, melted then cooled

3fl oz (75ml) single cream
6oz (175g) self-raising flour, sifted with
  ½ teaspoon baking powder

1. Separate the eggs and whisk the whites with the salt in a clean bowl until stiff. Add the sugar, a bit at a time, and whisk again until it stands in peaks.

2. Add the egg yolks, whisk again, then lightly mix in the butter and cream.

3. Use a palette knife or rubber spatula to fold in the flour. Try to keep the mixture as fluffy and light as possible.

4. Cut some greaseproof paper to the size of a 7 inch (18cm) steamer with a 4 inch (10cm) overlap, and butter lightly. Gently pour the mixture into the steamer, cover and steam for 20 minutes over boiling water.

5. Turn the cake out, cut into slabs and serve immediately.

VARIATIONS

✦ Another way of serving this cake is with a mango coulis or purée (take 2 very ripe mangoes and pass the flesh through a sieve or liquidise, with 1 tablespoon pure orange juice).

✦ Or serve it with Coconut Ice Cream (p. 156).

COCONUT ICE CREAM & MANGO FLOWERS

CHANDRA'S daughter, Neisha, was a very fussy eater when small, and seemed to survive on no more than a packet of twiglets a day. Even getting her to drink her milk as a baby was a major performance – one of us would have to carry her and dance around the room while Mother sang strange high-pitched songs from Chinese operas. If the baby approved she would deign to swallow one minute mouthful. If not, the whole palaver would start again until we were all exhausted.

Thank goodness Neisha grew out of her picky eating habits. She is now the family's official cake-maker and producer of desserts for parties. This is one of her favourite recipes and she makes the most beautiful ice bowls using not only flowers but herbs and fruit, too.

SERVES 6–8

1 × 1¾ pint (1 litre) tub of the best-quality full-cream vanilla ice cream (or make your own)

1 × 7oz (200g) block coconut cream, mixed with 1 tablespoon hot water
grated rind and juice of 1 lime
2 mangoes (ripe but still fairly hard)

1. Soften the ice cream, fold in the rest of the ingredients, except the mangoes, and put back into the freezer to harden.

2. Scoop the ice cream into small balls and serve in an ice bowl (see below).

3. Peel the mangoes. Then, using a sharp knife, carefully cut segments lengthwise to resemble flower petals. Use to decorate the coconut ice cream.

Making a Decorative Ice Bowl

You will need:

a handful of edible flowers
a selection of sliced fresh fruit with the skin on (e.g. oranges, lemons and kiwi fruit) or small whole fruit (e.g. kumquats or green and black grapes)

2 metal or plastic bowls of different circumferences, one smaller by at least 1 inch (2.5cm) diameter than the other

1. The smaller your inner bowl, the thicker the sides of your ice bowl and the longer it will take to melt. It defeats the purpose to have the bowl too thick and ungainly so experiment with plain water until you are happy with the result. Quarter fill the larger bowl with water and add a few flowers or slices of fruit.

2. Place the other bowl in this bowl, put a small cup or some other heavy object in it to weigh it down, then put the bowls in the freezer to set, making sure they are level. The water should only come about halfway up the outside of the smaller bowl.

3. Take the bowls out, add more water and flowers, and refreeze.

4. When ready to serve, take the bowls out, remove the weight from the smaller bowl and pour a little hot water into it.

5. Give the bowls a twist in opposite directions and remove the smaller bowl. Your ice bowl, complete with edible decoration, is now ready to be filled with a number of iced desserts, such as sorbets, melon balls or fruit salad.

6. Ice bowls only last for 2 hours or so in a warm room or in summer, so fill at the last possible moment, on the point of service. And, of course, you will remember to put your ice bowl on a serving dish which is deep enough to catch drips or (like one of us) you will find your buffet table very damp indeed!

VARIATIONS

✦ Add a few drops of food colouring to the water. Those who really have time to 'stuff a mushroom' can express their artistic leanings by using several different colours, adding only a little water at a time and tilting the bowl carefully between each filling and freezing. You will end up with a very beautiful rainbow-coloured container but this is so fiddly and time-consuming we only recommend it for very special occasions.

✦ Using soda water will ensure that your ice bowl is crystal clear.

MARSHMALLOWS

ONE OF our funniest memories was helping our cousin Pauline Smith to make a gigantic trayful of marshmallows for her parents' Silver Wedding Anniversary party. The only place to put it was on top of our fridge, but in our haste we forgot to cover the tray with a clean tea towel. When we went to see if the marshmallows were ready, we found that a little transparent lizard or gecko had fallen into the nearly set mixture. Determined to escape, it was executing perfect breast strokes, worthy of an Olympic gold medallist, but in extremely slow motion. In times of stress these little animals shed their tails which go on twitching for some time as a decoy. This one's was swimming off in the opposite direction. Pauline's rage was something to behold. Of course we had to start again!

1 × 1oz (30g) sachet Davis gelatine	9oz (250g) icing sugar, sifted
12oz (350g) white granulated sugar	food colouring (see below)

1. Put 2fl oz (50ml) water in a bowl and sprinkle the gelatine on top. Leave for 10 minutes to get spongy.

2. Pour another 2fl oz (50ml) water into a saucepan, add the granulated sugar and bring to the boil. Reduce the heat, add the gelatine mixture, and keep stirring over a low heat until the gelatine has dissolved and the mixture becomes syrupy.

3. Remove from the heat and leave to cool down slightly, then tip into a very large heatproof mixing bowl and beat with an electric whisk until very light, thick and foamy.

4. Divide into separate bowls and colour/flavour with any of the following combinations. For pink, use ½ teaspoon raspberry or rose flavouring and a drop of red colouring if needed. For green, use ½ teaspoon pistachio and a drop of green colouring. For yellow, use ½ teaspoon pineapple flavouring and a drop of yellow colouring. For white, use ½ teaspoon vanilla essence. Marshmallows are far more appetising when delicately presented, so go easy on the colours and flavourings.

5. Turn the mixture into lightly oiled flat baking trays and leave to set (about 9 hours or overnight) in a cool place or in the refrigerator. When set, cut into cubes or diamonds and dust with the sifted icing sugar.

6. Stored in an airtight container, the marshmallows will last for at least a week.

Peking Dust
PURÉED CHESTNUTS COVERED IN WHIPPED CREAM

THIS DISH is in memory of our maternal grandfather whom we never knew. A Manchurian warlord, he brought his five wives (our grandmother and four concubines) and 22 children to live within the gates of the Forbidden City. Do you wonder that the whole family was enraptured by the film *The Last Emperor?* Mum remembered well the hot, dusty streets of Peking in summer.

Peking Dust can be made up to 3 hours before serving.

SERVES 4–6

1½ lb (675g) raw chestnuts or 1 × 1lb (450g) chestnut purée
5oz (150g) icing sugar, or 1oz (25g) icing sugar if using sweetened purée

10fl oz (275ml) double cream
1 tablespoon icing sugar, to dust the top of the dessert

1. Cut a small cross in each chestnut and either roast or boil them until soft.

2. Peel them while still hot, then push through a sieve or put in a food processor on high until almost reduced to a powder.

3. Add 4oz (110g) of the icing sugar, then heap on a pretty plate in the form of a mountain. If using sweetened purée, omit the sugar and go straight to this stage. Taste and add more sugar if necessary.

4. Whisk the cream to soft peak stage with the rest of the sugar and carefully cover the chestnut mountain, using a knife to smooth the sides.

5. Use a fine sieve to sift a little icing sugar over the cream, before serving.

VARIATION
✦ Those who like to give their desserts a little extra pizzaz can stir 1–2 teaspoons kirsch (cherry liqueur) or other spirit into the cream after whisking it at step 4.

AVOCADO ICE CREAM

AVOCADOS grow to an immense size – larger than grapefruit – in the East, and more round than pear-shaped. Their flesh is also much creamier and softer. You may only be used to eating them as savouries, in salads or stuffed with prawns, but we would eat them sweetened any day in preference.

Because of the general liking for condensed milk in tea and coffee (we warned you of the prevalent sweet tooth here!), we would always have a tin of the gooey stuff in the refrigerator. Chandra would mix avocado with condensed milk and powdered milk to make a thick purée and we would sit in the branches of our guava tree scoffing bowlfuls. No wonder we were so plump as children!

This dish is not strictly an ice cream – more like a rich Indian *kulfi*. As with most of the recipes in this chapter, serve in small quantities!

SERVES 4

5fl oz (150ml) clotted or thick double
  cream
1 tablespoon sugar

2 large ripe avocados, weighing about
  1½ lb (675g)

1. Whip the cream, fold in the sugar and keep on one side.

2. Cut the avocados in half and scoop out the soft flesh. Be sure to scrape out every bit of the dark green flesh nearest the skin – it gives the deepest colour. Mash with a fork, then mix into the cream mixture. Cover and freeze until almost set.

3. Take out of the freezer and put in a food processor on high for a few minutes until all the ice particles have broken down.

4. Cover and return to the freezer until hard.

5. Scoop into small balls and serve with a sharp fruit sauce (see below) or very thin, crisp, sweet butter biscuits.

VARIATIONS

✦ You can make this dessert a little less rich by stirring in the juice of 2 limes at the point of freezing.

✦ To make a sharp fruit sauce to serve with the ice cream, liquidise 8oz (225g) raspberries, strawberries or blackcurrants with the juice of ½ a lime and put through a sieve. Add a little sugar to taste.

✦ We remember going to relations' houses and being served this recipe in its unfrozen state. It tasted divine and would sometimes be delicately flavoured with crushed cardamom seeds. Cover with clingfilm or lay a damp piece of parchment paper over the surface to exclude the air, and don't prepare too long in advance or it will oxidise and start to turn black.

BATATADA
PORTUGUESE POTATO CAKE

Rani's friend and colleague Larry O'Neil has almost as mixed a background as us! His mother is Spanish/Filipina and this is one of her own handed-down-the-generations recipes. Batatada barely rises and is a heavy solid cake but it is very delicious and has a lovely pale golden colour. It is found in many South-East Asian countries in various forms, thanks to the seafaring Dutch and Portuguese.

Larry says this is an office favourite and he makes it in at least double the quantity given in the recipe.

MAKES *a 7 inch (18cm) cake*

1½lb (675g) potatoes, peeled and boiled
2 whole eggs
2 extra egg yolks
4oz (110g) butter, softened

4oz (110g) self-raising flour
4oz (110g) desiccated coconut
8oz (225g) white caster sugar

1. Preheat the oven to 180°C/350°F/Gas Mark 4, and grease a 7 inch (18cm) cake tin.

2. Put all the ingredients into a liquidiser and blend well.

3. Turn into the buttered tin and bake until a skewer plunged into the middle comes out clean (1–1½ hours).

4. Cut into small slices and serve warm or cold with whipped cream if liked.

VARIATION

✦ To ring the changes, add either 1–2 ripe mashed bananas or 2oz (50g) crushed pineapple pieces or 1 teaspoon vanilla essence or rosewater to the above recipe at step 2.

Glossary

Agar-Agar – The vegetarian alternative to gelatine, agar-agar is made from various kinds of seaweed. Used in place of gelatine, dishes made with agar-agar possess a unique crunchy texture and will set at room temperature, an added advantage in the East where many households still do not possess refrigerators.

Allspice – Also known as Jamaican pepper, this fragrant berry combines the flavours of cinnamon, nutmeg and cloves in one spice. Equally good in savoury or sweet dishes.

Bamboo Shoots – Bland in taste, like bean curd, bamboo shoots have the chameleon-like ability to absorb seasonings, and will add a delicious crunch to stir-fried and braised dishes. Widely available in tinned form, they need to be drained before use.

Bean Curd/Tofu – Made from puréed yellow soya beans, tofu is essentially tasteless but possesses high protein value. It is sold in the form of white gelatinous cakes covered in water, and can be added to meat, fish or vegetables where it will absorb all the flavours of the dish. It can also be coated in rice or cornflour, fried and added to other dishes or it can be eaten by itself with dipping sauces.

Bean Sprouts – These are the shoots of sprouted mung beans or soya beans (p. 148). If stir-frying bean sprouts, cook for no more than a couple of minutes to retain their crispness. They also make a welcome addition to salads.

Besan/Chickpea flour – Especially good as a batter for coating deep-fried foods, as it sticks like glue.

Bhajii – A popular snack made from spicy onions coated in chickpea flour batter and then deep-fried.

Blachan/Shrimp Paste – Often used to give the familiar fish undertone to Thai dishes, this paste is made of dried shrimps and possesses a very strong odour. If the paste is wrapped in aluminium foil and grilled or baked in the oven for approximately 10 minutes, it will blend more easily with other ingredients. Use sparingly.

Black Beans – Salted soya beans commonly used to add a distinctive flavour to Chinese dishes. Should be soaked for 10 minutes before use to remove excess salt, then mashed to release the maximum flavour.

Cardamom – These fragrant little black seeds are encased in small green, white or black pods. They can be used whole or the seeds can be extracted from the pods before cooking. Used to add depth to curries and braised dishes. Also frequently used in cakes and sweets in the East or as a breath-freshener. We refer throughout the book to green cardamom pods.

Chillies – A common ingredient in Sri Lankan, Indian and Thai cuisine, chillies come in a variety of colours and shapes, fresh and dried, pieces and powdered. The general rule is that the smaller the chilli, the hotter the taste! The heat is provided by the seeds in the chilli pod and these can be removed from fresh chillies if a milder taste is required.

Cinnamon – The bark of the cinnamon tree produces this fragrant spice which is used equally in savoury and sweet dishes in the East.

Cloves – The pungent aromatic dried bud of a tropical tree, only a small number is required to add a subtle tone to savoury or sweet dishes.

Coconut Milk/Cream – The flesh of the coconut is grated and mixed with a very small amount of warm water to obtain the thick milk known as coconut cream. The same pulp can then be squeezed again, twice more, to make a thinner liquid known as coconut milk. Coconut milk is widely available in powder and block form (known as creamed coconut) which has to be mixed with hot water to get the consistency required. It can also be found ready-to-use in tins. Desiccated coconut is well known to Western cooks, usually for cake-making.

Coriander – The main spice in most curries when mixed with cumin and turmeric. Also known as *dhania*, coriander can be found as seeds, powder or as fresh leaves. The seeds can be used whole or ground and a stronger flavour is gained by dry-roasting them for 2–3 minutes over a medium heat in a heavy-based pan until they darken in colour. The fresh leaves are also known as Chinese parsley. The leaves should be kept refrigerated in a plastic bag and are easily grown at home from coriander seeds. Substituting dried coriander for fresh will not give the same flavour; ordinary parsley should be used in recipes if fresh coriander cannot be obtained.

Cumin – Cumin seeds can be used whole, ground or roasted in the same way as coriander seeds. Sometimes roasted ground cumin is sprinkled on top of cooked dishes as a final flavouring.

Curry Leaves – Also known as *karapincha* in Sri Lanka, curry leaves are an important element in Asian cooking. A few leaves added to any dish will impart a delicate curry smell and flavour. The leaves can be fried and crumbled into dishes for a more robust taste. There is no alternative.

Dhal – Lentils or pulses cooked with spices and served with rice or breads. A nourishing vegetarian alternative to meat.

Thosai/Dosa – Rice, lentil flour and spices made into a thin, delicious, savoury pancake.

Fennel – The flavouring agent used in liquorice. Extremely good with meat dishes to impart a sweet, fragrant flavour.

Fenugreek – These yellow seeds are used primarily to accentuate the flavour of lighter spices. Particularly good with vegetables, the seeds are slightly bitter and should be used sparingly.

Fish Sauce – Also known as *nam pla* in Thailand. Made from pressed salted anchovies, this thin brown liquid is often used instead of salt in Thai cuisine.

Five Spice Powder – A mixture of five spices, ground to a powder, commonly used in Chinese cooking. Consists of star anise, fennel seeds, cinnamon, Szechuan pepper and cloves. The pretty flower-like star anise provides the distinctive aniseed smell and flavour of this mixture.

Galangal – A member of the ginger family, galangal is used extensively in South-East Asian cooking. Pound in a mortar and pestle, grinder or liquidiser with a little water. The dried form of galangal requires soaking before it can be treated as above.

Garlic – Along with ginger and onions, garlic forms the 'trinity' required for most Oriental and Asian cuisine. The medicinal properties of garlic are now well known and fresh garlic, dried garlic flakes and powdered garlic are widely available.

Ghee – Clarified butter used for cooking foods at high temperatures where ordinary butter would burn. Easily made by melting butter and separating the clear clarified butter from the residue.

Ginger – This aromatic root provides a warm, spicy note in savoury or sweet dishes. Fresh ginger should be peeled and grated or crushed, or liquidised with a little water in a blender or food processor, before use. Can also be found in dried powder form, although this is not in the same class as fresh ginger. Ginger can be stored in the refrigerator, wrapped in clingfilm, or buried in sandy soil, where it will not only retain its freshness but will produce more shoots for use, if it is sparingly watered.

Hodi – A versatile Sri Lankan coconut soup customarily used to moisten Stringhoppers (see page 165) or as the basis of white vegetable curries.

Hoppers – Also known as *appa* in Sri Lanka, hoppers are a cross between a pancake and a crumpet. Made by swishing a rice flour batter into a small rounded pan (similar to a *karahi* used in Balti cooking), covering the pan with a lid and baking it, the edges of the hopper turn crispy brown whilst the centre becomes light and spongy. Often eaten in Sri Lanka for breakfast with an egg cooked in the centre.

Hoi Sin Sauce – A thick sweetish brown sauce made of soya beans, garlic, chilli and spices – especially good for flavouring barbecues and grills.

Jaggery – Brown sugar made from palms. Used commonly in Sri Lanka in place of cane sugar and, mixed with coconut, it is the basis of many Sri Lankan puddings and sweets.

Kaffir Lime Leaves – Often used in Thai dishes, these leaves add the distinctive aroma of limes. If unavailable, grated lime rind may be substituted.

Lemon Grass – A grasslike plant which imparts a delicate citrus flavour. Extensively used in Thai and Sri Lankan cuisine. Grated lemon rind can be substituted but will have a stronger flavour.

Lentils or Pulses – Also known as *dhal*, these are packed with protein and are the staple food of many households in the East. There are many different types of lentils, the commonest being *moong dhal* (the green whole grain is the mung bean used for bean sprouts, whilst the yellow type is hulled and split), *urid dhal* (black is the whole grain; white is split and hulled) and *channa dhal* (a branch of the split pea family and considerably larger than *moong dhal*). It is believed that the addition of asafoetida when cooking lentils reduces the unfortunate side effect of eating too many pulses – flatulence!

Maldive Fish – An essential ingredient of many Sri Lankan dishes, maldive fish is indigenous to the Maldive Islands, after which it is named. Flakes of this dried fish are used, like fish sauce in Thailand, to add a light fishy undertone to many dishes. If unavailable, ground dried shrimps are an acceptable alternative.

Mushrooms – The Chinese use a wide variety of mushrooms in cooking from button mushrooms to wood ear and straw mushrooms. Wood ears are a dried fungus and should be soaked for 20 minutes in water, drained, rinsed and have their stems removed before being sliced and cooked. Straw mushrooms are usually sold in tins and should be drained before use. They have a special affinity with crab dishes. Both these mushrooms are used to add texture rather than taste, as they are quite bland in flavour.

Mustard Seeds – Commonly found as black or yellow seeds, used to add pungency to many Asian dishes. Can be used whole or ground in a mortar and pestle or a coffee grinder.

Nutmeg – Although usually sold in powdered form, fresh nutmeg should be used for preference, stored in an airtight jar, and grated as required. The outer covering of the nutmeg is known as mace and this is exceptionally good in green vegetable dishes.

Oil – The best types of oils to use when cooking Oriental food are those which are not too highly flavoured, such as vegetable, sunflower and corn oil. Olive oil is never used in authentic Oriental dishes, as it is too strongly flavoured and is an uncommon ingredient in the East.

Oyster Sauce – A thick brown sauce made from oyster extract, sugar, soy sauce and spices, often used in Chinese cooking. Flavours vegetables particularly well.

Pak Choi/Bok Choy – A type of Chinese lettuce which is freely available for sale in Chinese supermarkets and easily grown at home from seeds, as long as it is well watered. The delicate flavour of this long green leaf, with its white central stalk, enhances many recipes and requires a minimum of cooking. Chinese greens (e.g. *choi sam*) and Chinese cabbage are also sometimes known as *pak choi*. If unavailable, Cos lettuce would make an inferior alternative.

Pandanus Leaves – Also known as *rampe* in Sri Lanka and used in all sorts of dishes, from biriyanis to curries.

Pakora – Small vegetable or meat pieces dipped in chickpea flour batter before being deep-fried.

Sesame Seeds – The seeds of this annual herbaceous tropical plant are used in both savoury and sweet dishes. The seeds can be roasted in a dry non-stick pan (for only a few seconds, as they burn in the wink of an eye) for a stronger flavour. Sesame oil is used for flavouring cooked dishes but rarely used undiluted for cooking, as it too burns very easily.

Sherry – Dry sherry is an acceptable substitute for dishes requiring rice wine although we tend to use sweet sherry more often.

Soy Sauce – An essential ingredient in Chinese cuisine, soy sauce comes in a light or dark variety. The light soy sauce is more commonly used in stir-frying, while the dark variety is used to impart a richer flavour to braised and slow-cooked dishes.

Stringhoppers – The Sri Lankan name for this speciality is *idi-appung*. Made from steamed or roasted rice flour, which is then laboriously squeezed through a mould with tiny holes, the result is thin rice noodles.

Tamarind – A velvety fruit pod, the liquid from the pulp is used to add a distinctive sweet/sour note to dishes. Most commonly found in dried block form, the juice can be extracted by soaking a 2 inch (5cm) piece in enough hot water to cover, leaving it for 30 minutes, then squeezing the pulp and straining the liquid before use. The residue of seeds and pulp is discarded.

Turmeric – The poor man's saffron, this hard yellow root gives a golden hue to dishes when used in powder form. Careful handling is required when using turmeric, as anything it comes into contact with may be stained a fetching shade of bright yellow.

Tung Choi – This is Chinese preserved cabbage and garlic shoots, known by a variety of names – Tianjin preserved vegetable (made from Tianjin cabbage), winter cabbage pickle or *tung tsai*. These savoury, salty, brownish flakes of preserved vegetable are usually sold in sachets or lovely little earthenware pottery jars. An invaluable addition to the storecupboard, *tung choi* can be used to give additional flavour to soups, fried rice, noodles, meat or bland vegetable dishes.

Index